Praise for *Small Axe*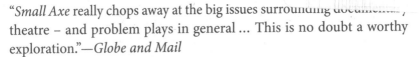

"*Small Axe* really chops away at the big issues surrounding documentary theatre – and problem plays in general ... This is no doubt a worthy exploration."—*Globe and Mail*

"Does the small axe represent the Black community chopping their way through the overwhelming power of a white world? Or does it stand for all gay people, Black and white, united in a hunt for equality? Both readings are possible in this uncompromising piece of verbatim theatre, which I guarantee will command your attention ..."—*Toronto Star*

"We all have our 'own shit' to deal with, our own biased blind spots to examine and challenge, and it's rare to see a work of theatre do this with such powerful swings as *Small Axe*."—*Torontoist*

"The best theatre prods provoke and inform. Writer/performer Andrew Kushnir's *Small Axe* does all that, and a lot more."—*NOW Magazine*

Praise for *Freedom Singer*

"A moving musical journey along the Underground Railroad ... with a *Hamilton*-esque twist: [the songs] are reinvented as hip hop, funk, and soul numbers."—*Toronto Life*

"Do we want to celebrate Canada's multiculturalist mythology or face darker facts about this country's racial history? ... *Freedom Singer* asks intelligent, open-ended questions and balances them with emotional musical moments and McClelland's indisputable musical talent." —*Globe and Mail*

"McClelland understands the importance of mythology and metaphor in creating a sense of home and place ... At a time when the idea of 'home' is so contentious, this is a sweet reminder of our own history of welcoming newcomers and the many ways people can stay strong in the face of tyranny."—*Toronto Star*

ALSO BY ANDREW KUSHNIR

The Gay Heritage Project (with Damien Atkins and Paul Dunn)

Hope in a Collapsing World: Youth, Theatre, and Listening as a Political Alternative (with Kathleen Gallagher)

The Middle Place (in the three-play anthology *Ignite: Illuminating Theatre for Young People*, ed. Heather Fitzsimmons-Frey)

Moving the Centre

Two Plays:
Small Axe & Freedom Singer

by Andrew Kushnir
and
Khari Wendell McClelland

WITH A CONVERSATION AND ESSAYS BY THE AUTHORS

Foreword by Cecily Nicholson

Talonbooks

© 2022 Andrew Kushnir and Khari Wendell McClelland
Foreword © 2022 Cecily Nicholson

All rights reserved. No part of this book may be reproduced, stored in a retrieval system, or transmitted, in any form or by any means, without the prior written consent of the publisher or a licence from Access Copyright (The Canadian Copyright Licensing Agency). For a copyright licence, visit accesscopyright.ca or call toll-free 1-800-893-5777.

Talonbooks
9259 Shaughnessy Street, Vancouver, British Columbia, Canada v6p 6r4
talonbooks.com

Talonbooks is located on xʷməθkʷəy̓əm, Sḵwx̱wú7mesh, and səlilwətaʔɬ Lands.

First printing: 2022

Typeset in Minion
Printed and bound in Canada on 100% post-consumer recycled paper

Cover and interior design by Typesmith
Cover image by Kyle Parent, Khari Wendell McClelland, and Andrew Kushnir.

Talonbooks acknowledges the financial support of the Canada Council for the Arts, the Government of Canada through the Canada Book Fund, and the Province of British Columbia through the British Columbia Arts Council and the Book Publishing Tax Credit.

Rights to *Moving the Centre: Two Plays: Small Axe & Freedom Singer*, in whole or in part, in any medium and by any group, amateur or professional, are retained by the authors. Interested persons are requested to contact Ian Arnold at Catalyst TCM Inc., 15 Old Primrose Lane, Toronto, Ontario, m5a 4t1; email: ian@catalysttcm.com; telephone: 416-568-8673.

Library and Archives Canada Cataloguing in Publication

Title: Moving the centre : two plays, Small axe & Freedom singer / by Andrew Kushnir and Khari Wendell McClelland ; foreword by Cecily Nicholson ; with a conversation and essays by the authors.
Other titles: Small axe | Freedom singer
Names: Kushnir, Andrew, author. | McClelland, Khari Wendell, author. | Nicholson, Cecily, writer of foreword.
Identifiers: Canadiana 20220135088 | ISBN 9781772013948 (softcover)
Subjects: lcsh: Canadian drama—21st century. | csh: Canadian drama (English)—21st century
Classification: lcc ps8315.4 m68 2022 | ddc c812/.608—dc23

for collaborators in life and art, who
make the big questions endurable

for Ancestors, who walked a long way

ix   **Foreword**
by Cecily Nicholson

1   **On Movement as a Practice**
An essay by Andrew Kushnir

17   **Small Axe**
18   Production History
18   Cast & Crew
19   Characters
20   Playwright's Notes

90   **The Passing of the Mic**
A Kind of Epilogue for *Small Axe*

91   **Inside of Another House**
A Recorded Encounter Between the Playwrights

109   **Freedom Singer**
110   Production History
110   Cast & Crew
111   Characters
112   Creators' Notes
114   Songs

185   **How Do We Get from Here to There?**
An essay by Khari Wendell McClelland

191   **Acknowledgments**

Foreword

BY CECILY NICHOLSON

There is something about a horizon that always seems new. The weather tempers the view with each iteration. The cast of light changes relative to the time of day or one's perspective standing on a dock, the shore, some morning of departure or evening after arrival. Our horizons may be just a narrow band of light at the end of a corridor of buildings that hover awnings and scaffolding in a cold winter, the steam rising through the sewer grates shimmering the way. In a figurative underground, we fold an allegorical dark into some light of possibility – new dawns we run for our lives towards. Between the two plays that compose *Moving the Centre*, playwrights Khari and Andrew wonder, "How do you know if you're doing or have done the work? Where's the line? Is there one?" and conclude, "I don't think there's a line. Or if there is, I think it's a horizon one keeps moving towards." This book contributes purpose and momentum in its movement towards new horizons, carrying forth work that cannot be tidy or linear as it sheds light on multiple encounters and collective processes undertaken by the authors.

These processes included successive runs of live theatre produced in multiple venues, impacting audiences in profound ways. As a reader I feel indebted to all the participants and contributors to the works-in-progress that led to these productions. This book is careful in its recounting and acknowledgment, helping the reader understand the genealogy of the labour. I am more than grateful for what has been given and sacrificed in the lead-up to this collection, which combines the original public works with individual essays, and significantly, a dialogue between Khari and Andrew recentring this and other necessary conversations. Regarding conversation, the authors ponder: "What's the conversation I want to be having? What am I doing, exactly?" And they agree elsewhere that "You can't have conversation if people's hands aren't busy." This work entrusts the reader with difficult stories that include experiences of gendered and sexualized violence, homophobia, racism, and stigma – and stories that pull through brutal conditions of slavery, as well as forced migration underpinning Black diasporic experience in the territories of the Great Lakes and beyond. The narratives propelling these works come by way of direct and mediated accounts homed in verbatim theatre. While I lift my hands up with respect, I also experience an immediate sense of entanglement – familiarity, concern, and willingness to invest in kind to the advancement of these important conversations. How will we busy our hands; how do we continue to diffuse power while furthering these conversations?

In whatever way you enter this book, the voice of contributor, participant, and character Jacqueline echoes. Her query, "Do you know what to do with these stories generously entrusted to you?," is interwoven throughout. This ongoing concern of the authors becomes a consideration for the reader as well. The title *Small Axe* is reminiscent of the African Jamaican proverb and Bob Marley 1973 lyric "If you are the big tree, we are the small axe." And as Jacqueline furthers in one of her lines, "The axe entered the forest and the trees looked to one another and said, 'Look, the *handle* is one of us.'" As the play and this book contemplate the risk of generosity, the costs of sharing trauma are tallied somewhat and met with responses that are honouring and caring, venerating without romanticizing, activating without prescribing. When it comes to dismantling and recentring power, the lessons are unresolved. Rather, it is the transparency in intent, and the vulnerability of foregrounding self and community critique, that is part of what makes this work such vital bricolage.

I am honoured to be invited to open a window onto this work, this assemblage of long-term and relational projects that, importantly, have become a book. A book, Khari notes, we can return to again and again for meaning: "With a book, I can find my own self in it, my different self, depending on when I pick it up." *Moving the Centre* provides opportunities to engage in verbatim theatre, in an oral history and presence that has contributed to critical interventions onto whiteness, class, and normative arrangements of power. All of this occurs with and within moving lyric, narrative, staging, music, and performances. The authors and collaborators bring documentary, record, memory, information, and events to the page, creating and holding space for experiences that have been lived. Throughout this collection, and, one can gather, throughout the practice of the participants, there is no shying away from questions, including big and complicated ones. Importantly, many of their lines of query, their searches and ruminations, have yielded questions that "could live inside of another house." This thoughtful framing of such iterative practices points to how concomitant works can be relevant and fluid while not necessarily having to be fully transferable or imposing in terms of structure. This critical counter to form resists colonial tendencies. Instead, these efforts share learning and understanding without assuming or imposing a specific tack or positionality. For me the inquiry-based approaches underlying these works provide a kind of pragmatic and prior infrastructure that adheres *Moving the Centre*'s narrative pieces together, even as each section can be approached on its own. The capacity to hybridize methods and outcomes has resulted in an inviting although unsettling text – unsettlement being a result I rather value.

The writers and performers consider how these works are not "tidy." As works that were already evolving, iterative, and organic during creation, it is unsurprising that a compilation of these efforts continues in book form to hold together somewhat unusually. No one has tasked me with creating an overarching summary melding five cohesive parts (two plays, two essays, and an intervening conversation) into a whole for the purpose of introducing this book. I assumed this might be part of my role here, but it isn't needed. Both authors' essays and their interim conversation at the heart of the book do some of the work of weaving common threads and themes that will assist the reader in understanding their relational aesthetics. I offer some words of introduction here as one additional tether to a body of work that can be read and engaged in dynamic ways. Voice, a rhythm and pulse, possibly even empathy, can be breathed back into text. Or a reader can just sit with the work, listen and witness, study what's learned, while unsettling one's place in and outside of it. We can approach this unconventional collection unconventionally, as Andrew notes in his opening essay:

> The zig and the zag of it feel right – like the way our eyes dart around a collage, taking in all the various bits that make a whole idea. This movement has some kind of relationship with verbatim theatre, this form of creating theatre from interview transcripts that have been sampled and pulled together, in often unexpected ways, to tell a story.

In *all that beauty*, Fred Moten contemplates the messiness of sculptor Harry Dodge's work as a form of generosity, noting the "the curvaceous pictoriality of Harry's drawing, or drying, or directing toward something culminating in assemblage," and through this practice how the sculptor, "bites into an earthly complication of the world." [*] Certainly, there is an art to these playwrights' "building a boat while on the waters" – hearing and adhering to adages and lyrics, lifting poetry up and outward from its quiet home on a page – surfacing weathered archives to set them adrift with new music and accompaniment. Numerous collaborators have contributed to an array of design, material sets, and thoughtful ephemera towards the public works underlying this text. This deep and fulsome outcome has evolved with complexity through time, stemming from early moments that were once simple sketches by individual writers. Any untidiness here is necessary assemblage detailing dimensional work that considers, in often poetic rumination, how to represent something of the actuals. In this collection, examples of vital, artistic, and musical storytelling cohere.

These authors work and worry about finding space and place to realize numerous possibilities for connection. Despite the profound and grating differences embedded in systemic structures and interpersonal troubles given ongoing oppressions, I believe they have enacted something generative here to that end. Striving to centre Blackness,

---

[*]   Fred Moten, *all that beauty* (Seattle: Letter Machine Editions, 2019), 103.

after Camille Turner's Afronautics,[*] these texts recognize time as non-linear, understanding that "silence speaks and yields information and direction, [and] imagination is a tool for building worlds." This critical book is aware of the facts. As futures for archives and arts, we recognize that "fleeting is the time" in all its human dimension. The "aura" and "residue" collected in these pages tell of ghosts turned into Ancestors, in works that are a testament to durational practice. Relinquishing fixity and ever approaching a just horizon, *Moving the Centre* reveals the journey itself as "a place to gather."

—CECILY NICHOLSON
December 2021

Cecily Nicholson is a poet, independent curator, and community organizer based in the Pacific Northwest. She was awarded the 2018 Governor General's Literary Award for Poetry for her collection *Wayside Sang*, published by Talonbooks.

---

[*]   See, for example, Camille Turner, Afronautic Research Lab, camilleturner.com/project/afronautic-research-lab/.

On Movement as a Practice

AN ESSAY BY ANDREW KUSHNIR

> Many Western traditions pin the arts against mortality;
> we try to make something that will abide, something
> made of stone, not butter. And yet theatre has at the
> core of its practice the repetition of transience.
>
> —SARAH RUHL, *100 Essays I Don't Have Time to Write:*
> *On Umbrellas and Sword Fights, Parades and Dogs,*
> *Fire Alarms, Children, and Theater* (2014)

This book has an order, but the sequence is the reader's to determine – whether you want to start with this first essay, or one of the plays, or Khari's essay at the end, or opt for the dialogue at the centre of this anthology. It's all fair game. As this publication has come together, I've been struck by both the accumulation of experiences and all the non-linear threads moving through this work, and my artistic practice, still. The zig and the zag of it feel right – like the way our eyes dart around a collage, taking in all the various bits that make a whole idea. This movement has some kind of relationship with verbatim theatre, this form of creating theatre from interview transcripts that have been sampled and pulled together, in often unexpected ways, to tell a story. It relates to my collaboration with Khari, our particular positionalities as people and as artists, but also the ways we have shifted each other's stories in both knowable and yet-to-be-discovered ways. I also see how it connects to a transformative era for Project: Humanity, the socially engaged theatre company that I've helped lead for over a decade now. Although "moving the centre" is a metaphor that came to me for different reasons (as I will explain), it does read to me as one that equally befits all of this motion and possibility.

Over fifteen years ago, Project: Humanity (PH for short) was initiated by a diverse group of theatre and dance students at Toronto Metropolitan University (formerly Ryerson University) as a way of exploring the possibilities of *artivism*. I appreciate the way artivism is evoked by philosopher and theatre critic Ileana Diéguez Caballero as "liminal scenarios, events when life and art, the ethical condition and aesthetic creation cross paths"* – and, in this vein, PH's early, grassroots activities ranged from artist-led clothing drives for local shelters to performing plays to incarcerated youth. Following its incorporation in 2008, the company's trajectory began to coalesce around two main things: bringing drama education into the youth-shelter system and investigating verbatim (or documentary) theatre as a way to more broadly "raise social awareness through the arts" (a first slogan for the company). Verbatim theatre was a way of creating performance that I had introduced to the company, although I was really discovering the form alongside them – something like building a boat while on the water. PH was at that time co-led by Antonio Cayonne, Catherine Murray, and Daniel Chapman-Smith – the collective that commissioned my very first verbatim play. *The Middle Place* emerged from two years of conducting interviews with residents and caseworkers at Youth Without Shelter in Rexdale, Ontario, one of the sites for PH's drama workshops. And it was this script that brought director Alan Dilworth and me together for a string of extremely formative years for PH's theatre practices and my own as a theatre maker. Alan's way of seeing theatre and its role in the world would spark countless hours of conversation between us, inform our four-year artists' residency at the Theatre Centre in Toronto, and ultimately provide me a bedrock for my first two verbatim theatre projects and so much of the work I've undertaken thereafter.

Alan was – and continues to be – particularly invested in the concept of encounter. As he puts it in his own writing: "There are multiple

---

* Gabriela Léon, "Artivism," Beautiful Trouble, accessed December 2021, www.beautifultrouble.org/toolbox/#/tool/artivism, translated from Ileana Diéguez Caballero, *Escenarios liminales: Teatralidades, performances y política*, Biblioteca de historia del teatro occidental (Buenos Aires: Atuel, 2007), 17.

human encounters in the theatre: actor and actor; actor and the audience; audience member and audience member. They all meet 'face to face.' Complex and often contrasting ideas, arguments, images, feelings and experiences are communicated in a theatrical encounter." * I don't know if Alan was aware of it at the time, when we started our journey together as collaborators, but verbatim theatre adds one further layer to the proverbial onion. Unlike the text of most plays, verbatim plays are typically composed of interview material – or what I've come to call *recorded encounters* as a way of reminding myself that this text comes from an interaction, a relationship between speaker and listener. What does it mean for an artist to be in relationship with someone in the world *on record*? How does that impact our sense of ethical responsibility to the stories we hear, as artists? Or our sense of care and accountability? Khari speaks more to this in the middle of our book, but these questions get to the heart of what is hopeful for me about verbatim theatre – that it's contingent on making meaning of the world *with someone else*. As playwright Tony Kushner puts it: "The smallest indivisible human unit is two people, not one; one is a fiction. From such nets of souls societies, the social world, human life springs. And also plays." ** Can verbatim theatre be an authentically relational way of creating for the inescapably relational space of the theatre?

---

*   This quote comes from Alan's excellent 2016 essay "Towards a Theatre of Rich, Poetic Language: David Latham's Image Work as a Way Forward to Creating Critically Essential Theatre for Our Time," in *In Defense of Theatre: Aesthetic Practices and Social Interventions*, ed. Kathleen Gallagher and Barry Freeman (Toronto: University of Toronto Press, 2018), 99–110. An essay of my own appears in this book too: "If You Mingle: Thoughts on How Theatre Humanizes the Audience," 83–98.

**   Kushner's quote comes from a 1993 essay entitled "With a Little Help from My Friends," originally published in the *New York Times*, wherein he tackles the "myth of the Individual." See, among other collections: Tony Kushner, *Thinking about the Longstanding Problems of Virtue and Happiness: Essays, a Play, Two Poems, and a Prayer* (New York: Theatre Communications Group, 1995), 33–40.

Alan brought to Project: Humanity – and me as a playwright – a wide range of other principles to consider. He helped me conceive of the theatre as a site for our democracy to work on itself. He spoke to how verbatim theatre could bring a plurality of perspectives into a space and thereby challenge the lack of nuance in our traditional forms of media, in political sloganeering, and in our social-media silos. And as much as this form could operate on the societal level, he helped me appreciate how it also provided opportunities for artists to personally grow through the expert testimonies of community members near to us and further afield. We can be – *and are* – moved by the words of others. I will never tire of pioneer documentary theatre maker Anna Deavere Smith's turn of phrase about the potential of her own plays: "to walk in another person's 'words,' and therefore in their hearts." * I started to see how theatre could be a process of learning something in public, a kind of witnessed practice that we all might grow from. And *practice* is the word (and another one of Alan's frameworks). I think we disserve ourselves and our audiences when we stand in front of them and report our findings. I've come to believe that it's incumbent on us to meet the ideas and problems and bottomless questions of the play anew, in the moment, together in the theatre. It's about the encounter. And it's something verbatim theatre can achieve in ways that other journalistic forms cannot.

This idea of practice helps me reconcile two opposing facts of the theatre: repetition and liveness. I often analogize this dynamic with my very rudimentary understandings of a yogic practice – how the poses are fixed concepts in a Sun Salutation, and adhere to a sequence, but the body responds to those poses differently each time one undertakes them. There is a newness in encounter, and re-encounter. And this can be a teacher. What do we gain from approaching a play, its order of words and movements and relationships, as predetermined, while accepting that the undergoing of those words and movements and relationships will feel different depending on the day we've had, the audience we've

---

*   Anna Deavere Smith offers a brilliant "Note on Casting" ahead of her play
    Twilight: Los Angeles, 1992 (New York: Dramatists Play Service, 2003), 7.

assembled, the historic moment we find ourselves in? We're also saying, in the theatre, *these words and movements are worth repeating tomorrow.* In this kernel lies my impulse to share *Small Axe* and *Freedom Singer* in written form. These plays, for me, do not embody conclusions or solutions, but rather represent a record of travel, of trekking over some complex terrain. They certainly challenge me to wonder about theatre's capacity to create public learning and/or learning-in-public. Even as I re-immerse myself in the original impulses, intentions, and impacts of the projects contained in this book, I am struck by how works of art are not a form of terminus for the artists involved. They are something we move through – particularly in the theatre and its signature ephemerality. In that respect, making a book about not just a pair of plays, but the ways in which those plays were made, feels strangely fixed. That said, I remind myself that published plays have an aura of sorts. They contain the want, the residue, and even the promise of *liveness*. And I'm buoyed by the possibility of readers engaging with them, having their own encounter in the now, formulating their own relationship to the questions Khari and I and our collaborators have turned over in our respective and collective practices.

∾

For me, this metaphor of "the centre" holds many potential meanings – which I like to think is the prerogative of a metaphor. When I turn it over, I see how it's the culture that is dominant among many cultures (a kind of central culture), it's the power imbalances that come with that, it's the way we've internalized these systems and hierarchies in our belief and value systems. The centre is the person or institution with resources; it is that which has been "authorized" to generate facts about people and the world. The centre is a myth that keeps getting reinforced. The centre is the city that has paved over hidden rivers. The centre is the self.*

The image of "moving the centre" came to me at one of the Walrus Talks on November 29, 2018, during a speech from poet and novelist Noor Naga.** In reference to her own work, she offered that an artist "empowers the voice of the centre by talking to it." I was troubled by this idea. Am I among the voices of the centre? And if not – by virtue of some calculus factoring in my being queer – was I speaking to "the centre" through my work, thus reinforcing its primacy? After all, "the centre" does reward us for speaking to it. *Small Axe* was incited by a specific interpersonal moment between me and a queer Jamaican Canadian friend of mine (the reader is welcome to zig to page 24 of this book if they want the fuller picture). Was *Small Axe* looking at the plight of Jamaican queer people (as the reader will discover) primarily for the edification and enlightenment of a white gay man and, by extension, of a white audience? Was it reinforcing the narrative that only through the pathos and transformation of a white figure can we empathize with issues that racialized people and communities contend with? By surfacing these

---

* In what is perhaps unsurprising to a verbatim theatre maker who overtly borrows from the world to make his plays, "moving the centre" is not an idea or metaphor original to me. But I didn't discover it until well into the process of creating this book and building on this key image with Khari. *Moving the Centre: The Struggle for Cultural Freedom* by Ngũgĩ wa Thiong'o was penned in 1993. In his opening essay – which gives that book its title – Thiong'o offers this line, as it pertains to African and Caribbean literatures: "It did point out the possibility of moving the centre from its location in Europe towards a pluralism of centres; themselves being equally legitimate locations of the human imagination" (p. 8). His point does not stand outside the core considerations of this essay of mine, and this book as a whole. I'd encourage anyone and everyone to connect with his writing (see, for example, ngugiwathiongo.com/moving-the-centre/).

** The Walrus Talks are a national event series "about Canada and its place in the world." Each Walrus Talk presents seven speakers who talk for seven minutes on a given topic. This particular evening, which happened in Toronto, focused on the future of the arts.

6

very dynamics, does something change? Can other valuable truths run alongside the risks of this work? I think I spoil nothing by saying that the play doesn't resolve these questions. As Khari put it to me after reading the play (he didn't know me back in 2015, when it premiered): "It isn't tidy."

I recognize the ways in which, over the years, I remain *in practice* with certain ideas and thinkers. Some of the quotes that populate this very essay are ones that I return to, again and again, in my thinking and writing about the verbatim theatre form. A long while ago, I was introduced to a quote (and dilemma) presented by critical race scholar Sherene Razack: "We (people of colour) are always being asked to tell our stories for your (white people's) edification, which you cannot hear because of the benefit you derive from hearing them."* Alongside it, I'm reminded of a quote from *Stamped from the Beginning* by Ibram X. Kendi – a book Khari introduced me to – that analyzes Harriet Beecher Stowe's *Uncle Tom's Cabin* in this way: "Racist Whites believing themselves to be void of soul, made it their personal mission to find some through Black people."** I then bounce back to Razack: "the difference in position between the teller and the listener, between telling the tale and hearing it ... To what uses will these stories be put? Will someone else take them and theorize from them? Will they serve to reassure everyone that Canada really is diverse and full of folklore? Who will control how they are used?" These questions both eat at and feed the heart of verbatim theatre for me – the extent to which stories are shared

---

*   This insight hails (as does the subsequent quote by Sherene Razack) from her book *Looking White People in the Eye: Gender, Race, and Culture in Courtrooms and Classrooms* (Toronto: University of Toronto Press, 1998). It appears in a powerful chapter entitled "The Gaze from the Other Side: Storytelling for Social Change," 36–55.

**   Ibram X. Kendi's *Stamped from the Beginning: The Definitive History of Racist Ideas in America* (New York: Nation Books, 2016) was a book that Khari and I listened to while driving to and from the Freedom Museum in Amherstburg, Ontario, on our first research trip together. The quote is from page 194 of that book.

with an artist, who then transports them into another context. I think of the profound care this requires, and the risks that coexist with this migration: appropriation of voice, appropriation of authority, paternalism, parasitism, serving the white gaze. Where is power located? And can we do more than speak to power but indeed shift the location of power in the theatre so as to not only imagine a more equitable world but build one?

It bears noting that all of these considerations and ruminations were not fully formed at the outset of creating *Small Axe* but were arrived at through the doing, the making, the sharing with collaborators and publics, working very hard to stay open to the response, however encouraging, harsh, or discomfiting, then remaking. The version of *Small Axe* published in this book (which is the production draft that was premiered in 2015) took shape through more than one crucible. Its first full iteration, shared in a public workshop presentation in September 2012 at the Theatre Centre in Toronto, elicited one Jamaican activist telling me, "Andrew, no matter how hard it gets, you have to show this play," alongside one close colleague telling me, in no uncertain terms, "I wish your play didn't exist." The question of permission (Is this play allowed, and if so according to whom?) has left its indelible mark on me and on *Small Axe*; for a long time, it felt like the central question of the piece. I came to discover that another question lay at the heart of *Small Axe* for me – a less binary one – albeit the heat of permission made it tougher to see. I don't think *Small Axe* is a piece that asks "Can we do this?" but in fact persists in asking "How do we do this?"

The first iteration of the play, shared in that 2012 workshop, hadn't created the space I'd hoped to make in the theatre. I had been seeking to orchestrate through my writing an encounter between my informants – mostly queer refugees from Jamaica – and the broader public. For too many audience members, I was getting in the way – not for saying too much, it seemed, but for saying too little. Following the second of two readings of the work, in a public feedback session, an attendee spoke up before the whole audience: "Why are you doing this? What point are you exactly trying to make?" I reflexively said that the play had shared my ideas, as they were developing, and I asked the attendee what they thought of the offering. I was saying, "I'm much more interested in what you think the point is." This audience member balked at the reversal. "I'm not going to answer that question. Why are you doing this?" As one of the actors in that workshop later put it to me, this audience member was "coming in hot." I was rattled. To my best recollection, I said that the play was an effort to understand an injustice in the world that troubled me as a queer man, but this was much more about me putting the room back together (and myself back together, in some way) than sincerely turning over the question in public. I don't remember what happened after I responded, but I'd be surprised if I at all satisfied the person interrogating me and the play. I certainly didn't satisfy myself.

I think this listener was reacting to a number of moments in that 2012 version of *Small Axe*. However, it's the climactic passage of that iteration that was the likely tipping point. I had figured that the most empathetic thing I could do in the play was to take that "walk in another person's 'words'" (as Deavere Smith put it). This meant that in the final "act" of the piece, I – as a performer in the workshop – spoke the words of some interview subjects like activist Gareth Henry, former gang-member-turned-artist "Flint," and Jamaican colleague and friend "Annabel," among other Black Jamaican characters. I did not affect a Jamaican dialect or character of any kind, I read the words in my own voice. My collaborators and I acknowledged that this would be a loaded action but collectively wondered if it might read differently given all the content and careful exploration that preceded it. I hoped it would serve as a metaphor – that an artist and queer person was attempting to make close contact with words outside their lived experience in order to better understand them. In essence, it dramatized the project as a whole – my efforts to comprehend the world through the words of others. An empathetic leap! And to some audience members, the action read as I had intended – a queer white artist trying to respectfully cross the borders of difference. To some, the theatrical gesture was confusing, muddling. To a few, this gesture read as a social and theatrical violation of great concern. This last response – one I suspect was held by the audience member who spoke out at the workshop showing – was one that I could not shake off.

Shortly after this showing, Alan and I postponed the premiere of *Small Axe* by a year. Those questions and criticism we were encountering around my positionality as a white person had me doubting the grounds of the project. Was my effort to do justice exacerbating injustice? I reflected a great deal on whether we had, in fact, created the kind of homonationalist piece of art that we'd been trying to avoid – which is to say, by examining or criticizing homophobia in a country (and nationality) that still suffers from imperialism and racism, were we contributing to that imperialist and racist oppression? I started to sense two distinct camps forming around the play. I had people (some white, some racialized) in my life saying: "But is inaction not tacitly supporting imperialist oppression? And is it not possible to act in solidarity with queer people in other communities?" I had a number of other people (some white, some racialized) fervently saying: "You're still not getting it."

For the longest time, I thought the work of *Small Axe* was located in speaking to the right people, finding the right stories and broadcasting them as truthfully as possible. That "getting it" and "getting it right" would put to bed the question of permission, and that it would raise social awareness in a rigorous and fair way. However, for all of its plurality of voices and viewpoints, a verbatim play does ultimately betray its author's sense of what is to be included in order to "do justice." And between 2012 and 2014, I found myself discovering in more and more vivid terms the limits of my compass, the limits of my seeing and understanding.

Prior to radically reimagining the play – which is what happened, and what is shared in this book – I had a visit with the very friend who had inspired *Small Axe*. I talked with him about all the trials and tribulations up to that point. I shared my doubt, my worry, my concern that the play was an impossible undertaking. Then I said to him, "Little did you know that the conversation we had all those years ago would spin out into all of this." And as it came out of my mouth, I became acutely aware of the extent to which I had seized something and run with it too far on my own terms. For years, I'd been striving to heal the world in some way, to make it easier or kinder for people like my friend, people who suffer at the intersection of racism and homophobia. It was the story I was telling myself – one that was not wholly untrue, but was certainly incomplete. What allowed me to rewrite *Small Axe* and navigate the question of permission required me to acknowledge that I was, in fact, trying to heal myself, my own being in the world, and my relationship to this friend. I was going to end up centred in this work whether I wanted to be or not – it wasn't a question of could it be avoided, but how could it be done in such a way that still foregrounded those I had spoken to. How was I to make their stories true to themselves alongside my own, as opposed to stories subjugated for my personal mission? Could I be the centre and move the centre from me? I not only needed to take responsibility for this challenging mission, but bring it into relationship with others. The theatre – whether by working with my collaborators or the play's audiences – was going to be the space to turn over this consequential riddle.

∾

Alan Dilworth once shared a story with me, that he had messaged a stage manager before a rehearsal saying, "Please start without me. I'm caught in horrendous traffic," and that the stage manager astutely messaged him back: "You are the traffic." To what extent are human beings prone to externalizing and objectifying problems because to do so keeps our narratives, our senses of self, intact? In what ways do we resist movement so as to maintain our sense of goodness, of order, of being outside the suffering of others?

The *Small Axe* that I reimagined after 2012 is dedicated and delivered, as a theatrical conceit, to the queer Jamaican Canadian friend who inspired the play. The audience is witness to that imagined encounter between him and me. In this regard, the play becomes a kind of letter that I deliver aloud (I performed myself in the production). I centre my Black Jamaican queer friend, but I address him with an awareness of the large number of white, urban, middle-class witnesses who would form part of the play's audiences. In other words, many people like me. When I look out into the auditorium, imagining myself speaking

11

to him, I am also speaking to them. This conflation is making *trouble on purpose*, to cast the audience as a queer Jamaican Canadian friend. I suppose I was exploring some version of Camille Turner's imperative: "I want people to see this familiar place in a strange way." * Drama theorist Ric Knowles puts it this way, when speaking to one of the key functions of art: "to make ordinary, taken-for-granted elements of life visible again by making them 'strange,' 'seeing things out of their usual context' ... and thereby seeing them 'as if for the first time.'" ** I hoped that this approach – speaking to a friend I had wronged – would be the most direct and transparent way of proceeding. I hoped that I was foregrounding that very thing the Andrew character first overlooks and then cannot unsee: his whiteness. Given the narratives, challenges, and insights of the racialized folx that I wanted to share in the theatre, it seemed incumbent on me to make whiteness visible (and judgeable). I had hoped, and continue to hope, that the opening line of the play could be dually disruptive – for the white audience member a moment of cognitive dissonance, of having their whiteness come to mind ("Wait a sec, I'm not Black"); for the Black audience member, a moment of being centred in a way that may not be anticipated given the fact that so much theatre favours a white gaze ("Wait a sec, is he talking to me?").

When I direct an actor these days, I've taken to asking, "What story are you trying to move us towards?" I came to this idea in part through the writing of theatre director Declan Donnelan, but before him (again)

---

* From CBC's *Art Is My Country*, season 1, episode 9 (see gem.cbc.ca/media/art-is-my-country/s01e09). An artist that I've had the great pleasure of crossing paths with – and even more so, one that Khari has developed a long-standing relationship with – Camille Turner is a performance artist who self-describes as "an explorer of race, space, home and belonging." She has incepted and explores a methodology called Afronautics. Among its chief tenets: Blackness is centred; time is non-linear; silence speaks and yields information and direction; imagination is a tool for building worlds.

** I came across this vivid quote in Knowles's book *How Theatre Means* (London: Macmillan International Higher Education, 2014), 43–44.

came Alan Dilworth. Alan once said to me: "In the theatre, language is made physical." I took this to mean that everything uttered is attempting to move someone from the story they're holding onto towards the story you'd like them to hold (including the audience). The centre, after all, can also be the self – our carefully constructed and often tightly held story of who we are and what the world is to us. *Small Axe*, in its genesis, looked to move some queer audiences away from a "post-gay" mentality – "post-gay" designating a world view wherein "homosexuality is no longer a significant social issue or a determining factor of cultural identity."* It looked to move some queer Black audiences from feelings of social invisibility into a place of prominence, of possible social recognition. That was admittedly a huge driving force for me. It also looked to move some Black audiences from a place of periphery to a context wherein their concerns ran tightly alongside a white artist's impulses and actions. And it looked to move some white, urban, middle-class audiences into a place of acknowledging their own complicity in the very social issues they pass judgment on (i.e., how do we call out injustices born of the very systemic oppressions from which we benefit?).

The primary tactic for all this movement, quite ironically, was a form of stillness. It was sitting in the dark together with voices and stories, and reconsidering how we receive them. A central question that Alan asked me in the *Small Axe* process was, "Is there a space between stories?" Can there be moments of being in the world with others where we resist the "zip" (our quick left-brain pattern-making) to feelings of either sameness or difference? Can relationships defy categorization, even for a moment? And what does this moment buy us? Is being in true relationship – or as Khari puts it, in "right relationship" – about listening in a new way? Is there a way to listen that challenges the camps of *us* and *them* so as to hear what's being said before it's slotted into a personalized proximity or hierarchy or value? Alan has a longstanding mindfulness practice – he founded the Stillness Room in Toronto, which he describes as "a coming together to experience the calming and quietly

---

* As defined on Lexico.com, s.v. "post-gay," accessed December 2021, www
   .lexico.com/definition/post-gay.

transformative qualities of stillness, silence and connection." I recognize now how Alan was invoking what neuropsychologist Chris Niebauer refers to as "something we could call awareness or consciousness ... simply the observance that the space is there." * Niebauer adds something that reminds me of when I performed myself in *Small Axe* back in 2015: "And of course, the left brain hates this, because as a lover of language, categories, and maps, it has reached the end of its ability to use its tools."

Alan staged the new climax of *Small Axe* (no longer did Andrew read the words of his racialized informants) in such a way that I would be rendered physically exhausted. What I recognize now is that he was driving me into the right side of my brain, the side that has some connection to compassion and grace (which has something to do with not attaching stories to ourselves so automatically). For me, *Small Axe* drills into how we might honour another's story – giving it the space it needs. It is the very crux of an ethical verbatim theatre. How might we listen in a better way – meaning more compassionately, more "globally," less self-centredly? I see how *Freedom Singer* carries that possibility forward, one in which a Black artist and his perspective stand at the centre, on his own terms.

I am indebted to the individuals – so many of them relative strangers – who spoke with me on record and shifted my understanding of self and the world. They entrusted me with their words and stories. My artist-collaborators (actors, designers, director, and stage manager) are just as deserving of recognition. They entrusted me with holding a space where they (along with their questions and needs) could show up in fulsome ways. And then there is Khari, who afforded me a next opportunity to carry what worked forward and to let further fall away those things that impoverish our relationships. How much of ourselves do we need to give up in order to really listen across the differences between us? How do we get closer to hearing what is being said? And how do we repeat this compassionate work tomorrow? Because we do tend, as human beings, to allow ourselves to be moved only to then

---

*   This appears in Niebauer's *No Self No Problem: How Neuropsychology Is Catching Up to Buddhism* (Boerne, TX: Hierophant Publishing, 2019), 61.

move back. I don't think of this as a failing, but rather as a feature of life that necessitates the art of re-engagement and reiteration. It stands as a reminder to me that we must keep practising movement, over and over, as a form of growth and change.

Noor Naga, also in her seven-minute Walrus Talk, recounted a concern her father had about her writing: "With writing comes a moral responsibility. And that in a few years' time, my ethics may evolve in contradiction to something I've already written. And at that point it will be too late to retract it." Her response to him: "This is in fact an aspiration. I always hope that my ethics are always evolving. Always slipping out from under my feet to meet my level of experience." She evoked for me something I'll call a *movement of ethics*. It feels counter-intuitive to me, insomuch as ethics are a form of grounding oneself, I find, a framework to help stabilize the tricky flow of human encounter. But it rings true to me, Naga identifying the ways in which we grow and change, and that our systems of understanding the world and how to approach deeper understanding move if we let them. I get curious about these plays as embodying a *movement of ethics*, the possibility of growth and a better relating. It is a movement that I can see recorded in the pages of this book, but, moreover, one that I can and must keep up in my life and living.

There's a saying, "The axe entered the forest and the trees looked to one another and said, 'Look, the *handle* is one of us.'"

—Jacqueline

Small Axe

Production History

Small Axe was developed between 2010 and 2014 in residency at the Theatre Centre in Toronto, Ontario. The piece was co-created by playwright and performer Andrew Kushnir, director Alan Dilworth, and Project: Humanity.

Project: Humanity's *Small Axe* premiered on January 21, 2015, in Toronto as a co-production with the Theatre Centre, with the following cast and creative team:

Cast & Crew

ACTOR 1   Lisa Codrington
(Annabel, Jacqueline, Cocoa, various Pride revellers)

ACTOR 2   Chy Ryan Spain
(Phoenix, Nicholas, Donovan, James, various Pride revellers)

ACTOR 3   Michael Blake
(Jonathan, Antoney, Michael, Maurice, various Pride revellers)

ACTOR 4   Sarah Afful
(Andrea, Lee, Claudette, Sunshine, various Pride revellers)

ACTOR 5   Marcel Stewart
(Flint, Gareth, Anthony, various Pride revellers)

ANDREW   Andrew Kushnir
(the interviewer-playwright, as himself)

Playwright	Andrew Kushnir
Director and Dramaturge	Alan Dilworth
Consulting Dramaturge	Karim Morgan
Set and Costume Design	Jung-Hye Kim
Lighting Design	Kimberly Purtell
Sound Design	Debashis Sinha
Movement Coach	Thomas Morgan Jones
Dialect Coaches	Laurel Paetz and Liza Paul
Stage Management	Michael Sinclair

Characters

ACTOR 1   ANNABEL, JACQUELINE, COCOA,
           VARIOUS PRIDE REVELLERS

ACTOR 2   PHOENIX, NICHOLAS, DONOVAN,
           JAMES, VARIOUS PRIDE REVELLERS

ACTOR 3   JONATHAN, ANTONEY, MICHAEL,
           MAURICE, VARIOUS PRIDE REVELLERS

ACTOR 4   ANDREA, LEE, CLAUDETTE, SUNSHINE,
           VARIOUS PRIDE REVELLERS

ACTOR 5   FLINT, GARETH, ANTHONY, VARIOUS
           PRIDE REVELLERS

ANDREW   That is, the interviewer-playwright as themself

19

Playwright's Notes

Small Axe is a piece of verbatim theatre. Apart from a few speeches by the character of Andrew to the audience, text has been drawn verbatim from carefully rendered interview transcripts. The encounters depicted in the play occurred between 2010 and 2014.

The play is written for six performers: five Black actors along with the interviewer-playwright. The five Black actors play multiple roles, which have been distributed through the ensemble in a deliberate way.

Many of the names have been changed to protect the privacy of individuals interviewed for this verbatim play. There are exceptions when individuals wanted to be identifiable.

In terms of punctuation:

- A slash (/) is used to mark the start of the next speaker's line (most often appearing before the initial speaker is done speaking). It makes for overlapping speech.

- A question mark between parentheses (?) at the end of a character's line indicates a moment of "upspeak," meaning that the voice's pitch goes up at the end of the sentence or phrase, as if to say "Know what I mean?"

- Bracketed numerals like (2) or (5) denote the number of silent seconds that transpire between spoken text. These are specific to the carefully transcribed interviews.

- A glyph (∿) indicates a kind of breath to be interpreted by the ensemble and director. These are deliberate "seams" in the play's construction.

- Other punctuation marks such as commas, dashes, and ellipses are at times used non-grammatically in order to best capture the rhythm of the original speaker.

The director and actors did not listen to the original interview tapes. This was done to maximize the anonymity of the subjects and to emphasize an interpretive rather than imitative practice for the performers. It is worth noting, however, that some characters speak in a Jamaican-accented English (Antoney, Maurice, Claudette, Gareth, and Nicholas). Other characters do some code-switching that activates a Jamaican-accented English on occasion (Annabel and Jonathan). The character of Cocoa speaks in a Trinidadian-and-Tobagonian-accented English.

Stage directions in the script come from the play's first production and were conceived in the rehearsal process led by director Alan Dilworth.

On director Alan Dilworth's production of *Small Axe*:

- On design: Jung-Hye Kim's set design consisted of a chair at centre stage surrounded by a large scaffolding structure. Actors 1–5 started the piece from elevated platforms on this scaffolding.

- On sound: The character of Andrew starts the play speaking his text into a hand-held microphone.

- On movement: In order to denote shifts in character, an actor would typically turn away from the audience (be it through a slow spin on the spot or a dropping of the head) and then turn back as the new character.

1: Andrew Kushnir, Marcel Stewart, Lisa Codrington, Sarah Afful, and Michael Blake: "Because this is purely anonymous, can you all come up with a, a pseudonym ..."

2: Sarah Afful, Marcel Stewart, Chy Ryan Spain, Andrew Kushnir, and Michael Blake: "I thought it was our story. I thought it was my story."

All photos by Dahlia Katz

Prologue

*ANDREW, the interviewer-playwright, enters the space
alone. He holds a microphone.*

*He stands in front of a large construction tarp, which
conceals the stage like a curtain. He begins addressing
the audience as an imagined someone, a friend.*
He speaks into the microphone.

ANDREW
You are Black.
I am white.
You are male.
I am male.
You were born in Jamaica.
I was born in Canada.
You identify as Jamaican Canadian.
I identify as Ukrainian Canadian.
We are both gay.
We are friends.

You are an artist.
I am an artist.
We are actors.
I am a writer.
You've told me you'd like to write.
You are well educated.
I am well educated. Formally educated. Whatever that means.
My mother's name is Orysia.
Your mother's name is Yvette.

Your name is one of the ninety-nine names of Allah. (I looked that up.)
It means "generous."
My name means "manly," from the Greek "andreios."
People tend to laugh at that.

Your skin is brown.
Mine is an almost olive. A little yellow in the winter.
Your hair is coarse, short.
My hair is curly, tangled.
When we sweat, we don't smell the same.

Years ago, while working on a show together as actors, we shared a dressing room. That's where you told me this joke:

A Canadian guy loves his wife so much – her name is Wendy. And he decides – he loves her so much – that, as an act of devotion, he's gonna get her name tattooed on his dick. W-E-N-D-Y. But when he's soft, all you can make out is W-Y. So him and his wife take a trip to Jamaica and he finds himself at this urinal, standing next to this Jamaican dude. And he looks down and sees the very same W-Y on this Jamaican guy's junk. And out of excitement, this Canadian says, "Hey! Your tattoo – does it say 'WENDY'?" and the Jamaican guy says "No man. That says, 'WELCOME TO JAMAICA HOPE YOU HAVE A NICE DAY.'"

Now, you and I have many conversations in this dressing room we're sharing. It's in this context that we become closer friends. And it's in that dressing room, one day, that you tell me a story. A story I've turned over in my mind, many times. Over and over. That's where all of this starts. For me.

You had been to visit relatives. Versions of this had happened to you before in Jamaica, in Canada. But most recently with Jamaican relatives in the States. You said to me: "Everybody kind of just avoided me. I didn't feel welcome, and I was there for a few hours and I was never offered anything to drink, not even a glass of water."

Your relatives had somehow found out you were gay. And that had changed your relationship with them. You proceed to tell me about this homophobia you've experienced in your community. You tell me about religion and machismo and going back home to Jamaica and not feeling safe in your own skin. You tell me that your younger brother had to defend you to relatives. And finally, you say to me: "I never get it, how people who have experienced the sting of oppression turn around and be homophobic. It's the biggest contradiction."

And I get excited. I feel incredibly close to you in this moment. Because I'm sitting there thinking, "Holy shit this is my story this is my story this is my story." Right away I tell you about Ukrainians. About intolerance in the Ukrainian community that I have observed and experienced. About religion and machismo and not feeling comfortable in my own skin. I say: "I never get it, how people who have experienced the sting of oppression turn around and be homophobic. It's the biggest contradiction."

You see: "My tattoo says the exact same thing."

But very kindly, very generously, you say, "No, my friend. It's not exactly the same."

After a beat, **ANDREW** *pulls down the construction tarp, revealing an extensive scaffolding structure that surrounds a single chair. Five figures stand on the platforms of this structure, their backs to the audience.*

ANDREW *sits in the chair.*

PART ONE

Same

ANDREW

First off, with these interviews I'm doing with people, if you were to give yourself an alias or pseudonym, just to protect your anonymity. (1) I'm happy to invent one for you down the road, but if you have a secret wish to be named after your childhood parakeet or –

> *ANNABEL laughs. She turns downstage on her platform to face the audience – as do all the characters when animated in an exchange with ANDREW. Until otherwise noted, ANDREW and the other characters speak (and listen to others) while looking out to the audience.*

ANNABEL

Annabel. (*laughing*) Here's the thing, right, if you're creating aliases, check with Jamaicans first because there, because they, there are very particular names: Antonette, Jacqueline, Jackie, Marcia, Andrea, Michelle, (*in Jamaican-accented English*) Simone. (*laughing*) There are these names – as soon as I hear them, you know it can be anything on the news, like some lawyer, I hear a name, I hear a name, like, I hear a name, like, um... Audrey MacDonald, and I think, "Oh yeah. She's Jamaican." There's something about, there's something very conservative and rhythmic about how – certainly with Jamaicans of my generation – about the names that their parents gave them. And um – so – yeah, there you go. Conservative and rhythmic. So be careful.

> *PHOENIX appears.*

PHOENIX
Do I want to come up with one? Oh... *I don't know*, I mean,
give myself a nickname. (1) To be honest, it would probably
be something really extravagant, like (1) Euphoria. (*popping
an eyebrow*) I don't know, I'm just, I mean, I'm being that
stereotypical homo right now but... um... (3)

Phoenix.

ANDREW
Phoenix.

PHOENIX
I like Phoenix. 'Cause I am fiery and always raring to go.
I am good.

ANDREW
And are you a reborn person?

PHOENIX
Reborn...?

    JONATHAN appears.

JONATHAN
A pseudonym? You want me to christen myself? (2) I don't know /

PHOENIX
Reborn...?

ANDREW
The phoenix born from the ashes.

PHOENIX
Oh. See. Now I've had a lot of thought about that and I really think that I could be that...

Each character, remaining on their respective platforms, turns towards the audience and offers their name.

JONATHAN
Jonathan.

NICHOLAS
Nicholas.

MICHAEL
Michael.

MAURICE
Maurice.

CLAUDETTE
Claudette.

PHOENIX
Phoenix.

JAMES
James.

COCOA
Cocoa.

DONOVAN
Donovan.

GARETH
You can use my real name. It's Gareth.

SUNSHINE
Sunshine.

LEE
Lee.

JACQUELINE
Jacqueline.

ANDREA
Andrea.

ANTHONY
Anthony.

ANTONEY
Antoney. Use m'real name.

FLINT
I would go with my first alias I ever had. Which was Flint.

ANDREW
Flint. Where does that come from?

FLINT
Um, (2) it actually, started off, I was like a little, um, wouldn't say pyromaniac but I, like, I used to like to play with fire.

ANDREW
Okay.

JONATHAN

Summer I graduated, I came out. (1) (*laughing*) Oh my God, um, yeah. Um. It was just after high school, when I was seventeen, yeah. It was really (*swallowing, quiet*) funny...

(*with a light laugh*) I wrote a letter, I was such a coward, I wrote a letter and I had a – I had all my bags packed, 'cause I was like, "Okay, well, everything I see on TV, like, you know, if you come out you die of AIDS the next month or you get hit by a car or, like, you get beat up or something, right?" So I was like, "I'm gonna die," so I was just, I got ready to get beat up by my parents and buried in the backyard, (*laughing lightly with what follows*) so I wrote this letter and I waited for my mom to come home, I think my dad was, he was working late or something like that, and my mom pulls into the driveway and she sees all my bags and shit. I gave her the letter and I kind of like scurry off, and then I'm like, I, trying to get out of the neighbourhood as quickly as possible, and my mom comes – I'm running down the street, right? I don't know where I'm going, like, I don't know how I'll get out of Yukon but (*laughing*) I'm just gonna go, right? Get out of here. And my mom, she, like, honks the horn, pulls up with the car, says, (*in Jamaican-accented English*) "Get in the car." (1) And I thought, "Oh God, here it comes, nobody's ever gonna see me again, it's over," and then she's like, "What is this letter?" She's like, "Okay, like. This is cute, like. But you know, we know you're gay, like, come on!" (*laughing*) And I'm like, (*laughing with:*) Oh! Such a buzzkill. I'm: "Oh really. That's it?" She's like, "You can go all, wherever you're going you can go, just, like, don't come home too late." And that was the end of that.

My dad, actually, it's so funny, I left and I came home really late at night, making sure, I knew they'd be asleep and I wouldn't have to see them. My dad was so cute, he left a little card on my pillow and I was like, "Ohh," telling me how he loves me and not to worry about it and a little condom, (*laughing*) a condom with the, in the, and I was, "That's mortifying." And ever since then, the joke is, I've talked about it with my mom since, but me and my dad have never spoken about it since then in, like, in terms, like, you know?

GARETH
In my childhood, I don't think being gay was only a feeling. I think it was a way of *seeing* also. (1) My grandmother never went to school. Never. (1) Nobody in my family ever thought to teach my grandmother to read. Or even to write her name. And at age eight, I taught my grandmother to write her name. It just dawned on me – I never saw her read the Bible, but she go to church. She sing the hymnal, but she ain't readin', she just know the songs. I never see her read *anything*. So I said, I said, "You can't read?" (1) just out of the blue, an' she said no. (1) An' I sit her down and teach her how to spell. To spell her name and write her name. Nobody in the family ever thought of doing that or concern about doing that. So when I look back on my childhood, I could see I was a bit different. Sensitive.

ANDREA
I had a friend – I had a very close friend, in university, who is gay – was gay, and when he told me he was gay, because all this time I knew him I had no idea, even though he's just like, flaming... (*laughing*) And... he told me that he was gay, and I didn't react well to it. Because I still had that, you know, that tape in my head saying, "Gay is bad." (1) And um, despite, you know, all my internal struggles, having crushes on my girl friends as a child and in my teenage years, but not really recognizing what that was about.

MICHAEL

I think, for me, from the time I was about ten, I was very conscious of, that I was attracted to men. (1) And, didn't have the language (?) or the, the... concept to sort of put it together. (1) And in the community that we lived in, in Kingston, we had two guys that were dancers, (1) they did ballet, and the expression... they were "battymen," right? Which is an expression for... gays, but they were *very* effeminate and (1) so (1) I knew that I was attracted to men, but I wasn't like them.

ANNABEL

Now listen, you should probably make it clear, contrary to public opinion, I'm not gay. (1) From what I've heard among the female gay population, even my best friend who is a lesbian tells me of these rumours, that I'm a closeted lesbian. A couple of my friends nicknamed me Narnia. (*laughing*) I know. Because of the wardrobe. Of course, I have dreadlocks, I don't wear a lot of makeup, I'm out there, my best friend is a lesbian, of course they say, "You're so deep in the closet, you're in Narnia." (*laughing*)

LEE

And, and myself, I've – for – my whole life even just gone, you know, as like that actor Alan Cummings, you know, "Are you gay? Are you straight? Well, homosexual or heterosexual?" – I'm just sexual. Kind of – and even Freud was saying we're bisexual, but even saying bisexual is... bringing the binary in, yah. So it's just: I'm sexual. Um, I try to stop commodifying – putting in boxes and drawing lines between, because there are no lines. It's like the idea of putting fences in the pool. Like, you know the water goes right through. I am Scottish on my mom's side and Jamaican on my father's side so – when does one end and where does the other begin, like, where does Jamaican end? What's Black? Like, you know, so we really have to get very, very modern, and stop being so binary. And so in terms of sexuality... there are people that I'm attracted to, people that I'm not attracted to, people that are attracted to me, not attracted to me so, so there's just, kind of just, I'm really one for taking all the things out and just going, "Okay, what am I in this moment? What are you in this moment?"

PHOENIX

I'm obsessed with being gay.

I... I just love it, I think it's... the greatest thing that has actually ever happened to me. You know, like, (1) (*inhaling*) 'cause I mean, most people wouldn't, and – wouldn't even dream – even some gay people I know won't... walk the way I walk. But I just can't help it.

∽

ANTONEY

So, I lived well in Jamaica. I lived really well. Um, I could afford a full-time helper, you know, this, that, live well. Live well.

Where I worked, right? In Jamaica, in my last place of work, it was the *crème de la crème* of society I worked with, right? Uh, not, not just locally but internationally – movie stars, heads of government, movers and shakers of all over the world, right? (*big inhale*) Um, so they used to (*starting to laugh*) call the restaurant the Fishbowl (*laughing*). It's an *aquarium*. 'Cause fish, when somebody call you a "fish" in Jamaica, it means you're a battyman, right? Get it? So it's an aquarium – it's a fishbowl. But I get to work in the morning, I jump out the taxi, and I do this (*demonstrating a strut*). I walk up the steps of my office (*demonstrating an effeminate and powerful energy*) with pumps! I'm coming down and some days I'm wearing pumps. (1) And they couldn't fuck with me.

MICHAEL

All through my college years, just really struggled, didn't date women, just had no interest. Struggled, struggled, struggled. And then, um, discovered porn, and so that became a bit of an outlet.

You know, sneak downtown and buy magazines, or once in a while sneak and get a video and uh, uh, kind of – but still not having the courage. And then here was this porn, here I am having these feelings, by then I understood what it was, I knew the language, um, having all these feelings, but I'm a Christian minister, right? (2) And really, really struggled trying to reconcile what I was feeling inside and what I, what, um, my professional call was. And (1) to the point where I started getting sick. Physically. And about once a year, I'd end up in the hospital... in severe pain, and uh, and it just went on and on and, um... Every year. Routinely.

ANDREA

When I was in church, um, there was a period there where – when I was struggling with all of that stuff, where I... sort of had one foot out and one foot in. You know, and both – like, I kept both sides a secret, do you know what I mean? From my friends outside the church, I didn't tell them I went to church, and from my friends in church, I didn't tell them that I did all these other things that I wasn't supposed to be doing. And that was a very disquieting place for me, and I decided when I left church I was never gonna go back there. So... I came out.

Um... my sister – everybody was fine, my mom still doesn't know. (3) She's in her eighties.

NICHOLAS

You know, with my aunt and uncle, my uncle would always make negative comments about... the gay people he would encounter. I don't recall my aunt saying... my parents, I don't recall anything negative. Never negative.

ANDREA

With my family. Maybe it's about their... their own fears of, you know, not so much that Mum wouldn't be able to handle it, but, trying to shield her from whatever sense of disappointment or whatever that they think she might experience, because that's maybe what they are experiencing, I don't know. (4) I don't know. We have a tendency to project, right? Our own stuff onto other people, so ... But knowing what I know of my mum, you know, my mum is a lov– she has met ... almost all of my girlfriends. And she has known that I've been living with a ... you know, a, she – I've lived with a couple girlfriends in my time. And, you know, so she's always known that. You know, and she'll phone, and she'll ask after them, because she lives in Calgary, still – she – you know, every time we talk, "Oh, say hi to so-and-so," or, "How is so-and-so," you know. So – and then she'll ask me, "When are you getting married?" (*laughing*) You know what I mean? In the same phone call. (*continuing to laugh*) So, so ... (2)

She has chosen not to acknowledge it. (1) And that tells me something.

~

NICHOLAS
I ... I didn't socialize a lot in Jamaica.

I was bullied, in high school, about being gay, people thought I was gay, they were convinced I was gay. And so I never went out, after ... my second year in high school, I was told, "If, if we saw you, out, we would kill you." (*light laugh*) Now, at thirteen or fourteen, I, had no ... way of knowing whether that was true or not, right?

It – it got so bad at school that I wouldn't go to the canteen, to buy a lunch, I'd have a friend do it, or I'd pay him to go and buy my lunch, or I would not ... eat lunch, like, I would wait until they ... had had lunch and then I would buy a chocolate bar o– 'cause it was quick and easy to eat and I wouldn't have to line up in a, in a certain line. It's an all-boy school and, you know, sometimes you need to go pee. I didn't want to go pee, I didn't want that threat of, (1) "Oh my God, Nicholas is coming to look at us." You know, "Look at the battyman." Um... nevertheless, I did, I do remember, uh, we had a teacher that came, in that... same year, that I... that was, that was... gay. He was (1) very... he was more effeminate than the usual men. The typical man. This teacher (1) spoke, had that sort of, (1) he had, he had, *he* had an upper-class accent, (1) uh, and I remember (1) writing a letter, and sticking it in a text – stick, sticking it in a textbook – telling him how much I like him, I thought I was gay as well, um, but I said that – I changed my handwriting – and said that I was in a different class.

Um, and... Andrew, I don't know what on earth possessed me to do this (*laughing*) and stuck it in the book, and then we had to, ah – he would collect the books, at the end of, like, there was forty students in the class, he would collect the books from us, and (2) and the time came for us to – we're in the class, and the time came for us to send the books up, and I sent the book up, just given it up, and uh – the le– the letter was hidden in there, and (1) the book didn't – I was, I think there was another guy behind me, all of a sudden I hear, "What is this?!" (1) and (1) somebody's reading the letter that I had written and stuck in the book. (1) And I, of course everybody turns to me, 'cause it came from either me or the guy behind me, (1) and, I'm like, I don't know, "What could this be?" Oh my God, like, and he's reading the letter out loud, and of course the teacher, mm – the, the teacher he is, *he's* beside himself, 'cause he's going, "I don't know what the hell to do now." I'm freaking out inside. The principal was called in. I don't know, I don't know how I managed to – like, I was like, "This is not from me." And then the the the the the book, I was like, "I didn't even, like, this isn't my b– like, I didn't write this letter, I didn't really check, I didn't really read the book." And I *had* written that I was in another class. Or I had written, you know, "I'm in 2F instead of 2D." (*long inhale*) Yeah, well it – ju– that targeted another guy, (*laughing*) which I was, you know,

I was fully behind. I was like, "Must be, 's not me." (1) But, the –
certain boys were convinced that I wrote the letter.

⁓

FLINT
Um... (4)

Um... to be honest, since this is, like, totally, um... so to be
confidential... my brother is actually a homosexual. And the first
time I found out about it... I actually, because I was, like, the
prominent man of the house, I actually had him kicked out of
the house. Yeah. Mm-hm. (2) He's like thirty years old... under
my parents' roof... living this secretive lifestyle and lying about
it. (2) I exposed it to my parents and they were just, like, pretty
much sugar-coatin'-denying it, even though he would carry a
lot of feminine features, and like, I just realized, "Enough is
enough" kind of thing, you know... And I was just taking the
responsibilities that a father should, you know?

PHOENIX
He, um, all my life, I guess he's been in denial and he's been trying
to push me... towards being straight, and always, every minute
he's, he's always like, "Oh look, at that girl walking down the
street," or, "Look at her breasts," or, "Look at her ass," or, you know,
"Think about her fat," (1) duh-duh-duh-duh, like, really things that
I'm just kinda, like, "Wow, *you're my father*, please stop."

FLINT
Last time I heard he, like, he got beat up by someone, you know...
for being a homosexual. Or someone, I don't know, 'cause, he's
really, like, an argu'tive person. So... last time I heard, he got
beat up, but he, I believe he's living on his own, he's okay. Mm.
(*nodding*) I don't worry about him. (*shaking his head*) Because we

were never close (?). We never had that, like, brother-and-brother relationship...

MICHAEL

I remember, um, the last three years of coming out – it took me three years to come out – and I was still in the congregation and, you know, knowing that I wouldn't last, um, and every Easter, while I was in the congregation, I ended up in the hospital. Routinely. I would do Palm Sunday, get through Palm Sunday, Monday of Holy Week I would start getting sick and, um, by Wednesday I was in hospital with surgery, and it was surgery related to – the surgery they had done to take my colon out. And um, you know, for three Easters I wasn't in church. (3) But I remember the first Easter after I came out, I met this guy and, uhhh, (1) you know, did, did the online thing, met this guy online, went over to his place and it was, um, (1) Holy Saturday (1) and, um, you know, and, I mean, (1) the sex was so amazing, I mean, I was in tears. (2) 'Cause – and – he didn't know what was going on, but for me it was just like, "Wow, (1) this is everything I dreamed this would be and, um, I never could have imagined." First time I'd ever slept overnight with a guy and, um, that next afternoon went to church. And that Sunday I was like, (*long laugh, four beats long, then an inhale*) Resurrection.

PHOENIX

I like Phoenix. 'Cause I am fiery, and always raring to go. I am good.

ANDREW

And are you a reborn person?

PHOENIX

Reborn...?

ANDREW

The phoenix born from the ashes.

PHOENIX

Oh. See now, I've had a lot of thought about that and I really think that I could be that...

ANDREW

And what would you say is the fire? Can you say?

PHOENIX

The fire?

ANTONEY

Ten years ago, I moved to Canada, nine years ago, but ten years ago, I was at work, uh, and somebody called and said someone is breaking into your house. "Okay. I can't leave. The owner of the business is not here, I cannot leave, I have to stay." So, I said, "Okay, I'll call the police." I called the police, police went. Um, called the guy who works at night, I said, "Hey, you better show up for work early because I've got to go." He was like, "Something's wrong?" I said "Yeah, they're breaking into my house and I cannot leave, so you better come to work early." Um, he came in early and – and left, went home, they – the windows were broken – the grills was broken off. They went in and took furniture, my liquor, all my jewellery, I had a couple of thousands of dollars in one of my drawers in my office. They got to it. Like, they were like, it's – all my appliances, blah, blah, blah, blah, blah. On the wall, in my living room, it says, "Get out of here. We don't want your kind in our community. You don't leave, we'll burn the house down."

ANDREW, who had been seated during all the previous encounters, stands from his "listening chair" for the first time.

ANTONEY

Um, I was scared, I was scared of calling the police. So – in the night there's some – I'm staying home. I went to bed and exactly two o'clock in the morning – they – the window panes in my room were broken with stones. They started throwing stones in my window, breaking the glass. I was lying there on the floor for a little while. I smelled smoke. There's a fire! The house was set on fire. With me inside.

GARETH

I became the leader of J-FLAG in December 2004. The Jamaica Forum for Lesbians, All-Sexuals and Gays. A group of gay men and lesbian professionals (they were mostly lawyers and doctors an' those people) decided to come together an' to form a group that would advocate for gays and lesbians and that kind of stuff. In the past, the organization had always been lead by a person who is not Jamaican and who is white. And so even though it was founded by mostly, 90 percent Black Jamaicans, it was never lead by. There was Brian, white Canadian. There was Micheal, who was from the UK. There was Tony, from US. Also a woman, from the US. Always not our colour. So I volunteered.

ANTONEY

I could tell you stories – you can change the whole script that you have in order to get a different one.

GARETH

(*inhaling*) In the four and half years that I was involved – actively involved with J-FLAG, thirteen of my friends were killed. And thirteen (*increasingly louder*) is a lot of people. You know, to lose one person is so hard. An' it's a great loss. But to do, to do that, go through that process thirteen different times, you know, it's, (*tsk-tsking*) it's not easy.

I remember Victor Jarett, he was beaten by police and then turned over to a mob.

I remember Steve, he was shot in the head – Steve was my co-worker. I had to go identify his body and the police called me faggot, battyman while I did it.

One of the guys, we went to his funeral, uh, Derek. You know, he was, um, you know, it was, um, he was killed. Um, and we, (*inhaling*) we tryin' to bury him (1) and we were in the church and everything, and, they were doing the passages and his whatever, his, uh, his sermon an' all of that stuff, and the church came under attack. They, the, the mob came into the church an' um, started to, to pull the casket outside cause they were gonna burn the body – an' they said that they want the body to burn, and no gay man is to be buried, gets to be in a church in the community. And um, that's what they wanted to do.

For the first time, ANDREW turns around and looks at one of his interview subjects directly. GARETH returns the eye contact, briefly, then turns away. ANDREW is left alone.

ANDREW
Do people know about this?

Are people talking about this?

A shift as ANDREW addresses the audience again, his imagined friend.

ANDREW
Your relatives had somehow found out you were gay. And that had changed things. And in the dressing room we shared, you proceed to tell me about this homophobia you've experienced in your community. About religion and machismo and going back home

to Jamaica and not feeling safe in your own skin. And finally you say, "I never get it, how people who have experienced the sting of oppression turn around and be homophobic. It's the biggest contradiction." And I get excited. Because I'm thinking, "Holy shit this is my story this is my story this is my story." Right away, I tell you about Ukrainians. About intolerance in the Ukrainian community that I have observed and experienced. About religion and machismo and all these things that you mentioned. I say, "I never get it, how people who have experienced the sting of oppression turn around and be homophobic. It's the biggest contradiction."

You see, I thought: My tattoo says the exact same thing.

But very kindly, very generously, you say, "No, my friend. It's not exactly the same."

PART TWO

Different

ANDREW remains standing, facing the audience,
listening to his interview subjects as they speak.

MAURICE

Initially, being a privileged, middle-class person, I thought these
stories couldn't be real. This level of abuse and intolerance
couldn't – because I wasn't personally experiencing – I mean, I knew
there were limits to my expression in Jamaica, but I didn't have the
sense that things were that bad for LGBT. Anyway, um, so, it was
recording stories after stories – and I tell everybody that I'm glad I
have a poor memory sometimes because... some of them were so
horrific, if I were to dwell on them, I think I would go crazy.

FLINT

Okay. Um, to me Jamaica always will be Jamaica, that's just the
way the media portrays Jamaica as. Um, the violence is nothing
new, right?

Like, *I seen the guns* when I went there, like you know. So, that
stuff is nothing new, but... when people go there, they often stay in
the tourist section, right, which is pretty much like a total different
world from outside that area, so –

Um, but right now they, like – the media they show it as, like,
as a country in chaos. And it is in chaos, but they don't show you
why they're in chaos, you know? *Why* they're in the position that
they are.

MAURICE

I eventually just asked my mother … why does she think Jamaica is this homophobic. And she shared that in her small village, where she grew up, everybody knew somebody who was gay, wasn't talked about, wasn't anybody's business, there were gay couples, it was live and let live, nobody cared. And as long as you contributed to society, you were fine. But then during the eighties, the late seventies and eighties, we started to see the import of televangelists. From North America.

And they were particularly, I mean, horrid – horrid, horrid in terms of the messaging. I remember going around the house turning off TVs 'cause – my dad used to hate it – he thought he was doing his Christian duty by keeping them on twenty-four hours a day – we'd have religious stuff blaring and I thought, "This stuff is *hateful*."

FLINT

History has a big part of – yeah, that's one thing I forgot to mention, about Jamaican history. Jamaica was where a lot of, um, rebellious slaves went. And that's why they're portrayed as a really violent place, because a lot of the slaves that rebelled, like, comin' across the transatlantic ocean, went to the Caribbean. Specifically Haiti and Jamaica. So we, as Jamaicans, we always knew how to stand up, kinda thing.

MAURICE

And um, my mom admitted she saw, in her words, "society started to coarsen." So even our music started to coarsen. You know from Bob Marley (*singing*) "One love …" half-stoned, (*laughing*) you know … feel-good music … to the most horrific – not only anti-gay but misogynistic, just *bad*. It's been called Murder Music, these dancehall artists spewing this hateful stuff. And we realized that a lot of the youngsters singing those songs would have been in church – and they would listen to this stuff by the pastor or – and

they just became hardened. And that, I think, is where it started.
I honestly believe so.

DONOVAN
Now it ain't gonna be pretty, but we should talk about *plantocracy*.
'Cause that's a part of this thing you're trying to understand.

The masters, uh, you know, not across the board, but masters
raped... everyone. Women and men. And children. Their own
children. Let me tell you something. (*incredulous exhale*) We'll
talk about plantocracy. (*laughing*) But it's raping in many senses,
not just physically, but you know, you get older and you just start
to identify certain things, like, things start to fall in place. For
example, it's controversial still within a lot of Black families to have
long hair, for men to grow their hair, when I was little and I said,
"I think I want dreads because I like the look of them," and my
mom who's wonderful and loving, my mom said, "Okay, where you
going to live?" – (1) because it's such a taboo. Hair is a taboo, but
we Black people didn't get up one day and as a collective decide it
was a taboo, it's something we were taught.

If men were being raped during slavery, it was a practice of
demascunalizing them or humiliating them. Who knows, maybe
the masters got off on it too. Probably. But the point is, what does
that do to you culturally, over time? How does that make you feel
about men having sex with men? Just, generally.

Now, does everybody know about this in my community? I don't
know. Would it make a difference if everybody knew? Probably
not. Probably you'd get a lot of imposition and you'd get...
I wouldn't even touch it. It's too much of a – I wouldn't touch it.
The word "rape" alone evokes too many emotions.

~

ANNABEL

I remember, um… uh, things, funny things remind me about
Jamaica, um, (*laughing with what follows*) interestingly enough
one of them has to do with a white woman I worked with, she
came in one day (*inhaling*) and she, she had, she had put on *some*
kind of scented something, um… it was lotion. And it had this
smell to it, I think it was roses or something, and I said, "That is
nice-lady lotion." (*laughing*) "That's, you smell like a nice lady,"
'cause I remember going to church and these nice ladies with their
mantillas and their dresses that were cut (*chin down*) to right here,
and the sleeve was right here and the hem was right here and the
shoes were just so and the hymn book was just so and the Bible
was just so and the purse was just so and they'd say, "Hello Mrs.
So-and-So" and "Hello Mr. So-and-So," and then they'd look at us
kids as though we were the scum of the earth (*laughing*) and all we
needed to do was sit down and shut up and go up for our blessing
when, when we were called, and they always had nice-lady lotion,
nice lady – and they didn't sweat, or if they sweat it was… (*fanning
herself with her hand*) I don't know, there was some – *they* don't
sweat like *I* sweat. Like, I sweat like (*tracing big half-circles under
her arms*). No, didn't (*while ANDREW is laughing*) sweat like that.
I'm *sure* they were going through menopause at the time but it was
just, (*fanning herself*) you know… it was very, um… it was very
controlled. You, you didn't, you, you, you didn't bring that stuff out
for airing. (*shaking her head*) (4)

You know, the church, the church has decided that homosexuality
is not normal, um, the, um… popular culture has decided that
it's not normal and – the, the thing that gets me about those two
enclaves is that they are, in Jamaica, (*quick inhale*) they often exist
on… completely… as polarities, in relation to each other. And…
(*little laugh*) and this must be like, the *only* thing that they agree
on. And they're *both so* powerful that… you… most people belong

to one or the other... and... and um, and so, you have, you have, these huge forces, and there isn't much in between, you know? And if you're somewhere in between, then just so you're able to go through your life with some degree of comfort and community, you're going to lean to one or you're gonna lean to the other.

ANDREA
I wouldn't say – I wouldn't say I necessarily agree fully. But... I think the religious factor in Jamaica overrides all of it.

FLINT
Jamaica is a poor country. An' it's being kept poor.

ANDREA
Things have just gotten really bad there, so... there's increasing safety issues for *everyone*, not just gay people, and, um... people struggle, you know? The economy's a mess (?). Oh my God. (*laughing*)

But then you have the Church, see, amidst all that, the Church is there for people. In Jamaica, the Church is a source of money, loans, it gets and keeps families going. It is central to culture, to community. And so, yes, some of the doctrine is hateful. But like with most things in life, it's a trade-off. My mother has always said to me, "The Church will be there. If nothing else, the Church will be there." And so how can I blame her. That's been her salvation. And for her, real salvation is in the community.

NICHOLAS
The gay community in Jamaica is very underground. Um, and there's definitely a social-status divide with it. Within it. So, I'll just say upper and lower class, though that's being very concrete.

MAURICE

We have the law, from 1864, which criminalizes male same-gender intimacy. It's a colonial leftover – and there have been opportunities to repeal the law – and every time it's met with massive protests.

NICHOLAS

And the upper... One community does not want to socialize with the other. There's conflict between this upper and lower within the gay community itself.

MAURICE

And here you have this law still on the books, which in theory persecutes *all* homosexuals in Jamaica. But it's about class, right? With this issue, you can't forget about class. If you have money, when you're rich enough, you can insulate yourself from the violence.

ANNABEL

More and more men are starting to demand their rights and men with, um, with waxed eyebrows and sculpted faces and, you know, rolled up shirts and, you know, very tight jeans are walking around New Kingston shamelessly and the reaction to that is to... quash it. And so you hear about it more.

ANDREA

What it comes down to: It's an abomination to God.

DONOVAN

But you know, like, Andrew, like, every person, I mean this is – like every religious tradition –

ANDREA
There are at least a thousand murders in Jamaica every year, even though the Bible says, "Thou shalt not kill" – but the gay thing, it's not seen in the same way.

DONOVAN
Like every religious tradition, there are elements of hypocrisy in every religious tradition.

ANDREA
And why is it considered the worst sin? I don't know. I don't know, and this is a question you might want to pose to a theologist or something.

MICHAEL
It's a complex issue that's going on.

The thing I grieve about the discussion, if you look at it, every culture that is oppressive around same-gender relationship are somehow oppressive because somehow their religious literature has shaped their imagination around it. And mostly influenced by Christian tradition, as Christianity moved across the globe in earlier times. And a lot of it is a misreading of the text –

DONOVAN
The thing I grieve about the discussion is that we know it's bad – okay, we all know it's bad and where it comes from – but what is the appropriate intervention?

ANNABEL
The thing I grieve about the discussion is that you're not going to hear from the other side of this very much. With you're being gay and white, will they... I don't know.

ANTONEY

The thing I grieve about the discussion is that people think it's happening *over there*. I often say to people, when you arrive at Pearson International Airport, or wherever you may have landed from whichever port you're coming from – it doesn't mean you automatically... transform, right? You come and you still have all that prejudice and culture and learned things and indoctrination and dogma, you know, all of that baggage you take with you, right? – you don't just click a button – and bap! it releases, you're this new person. Like, you're taking a fart or something, you know what I mean?

ANTHONY

I'd like to say something. What I grieve about the discussion. (4)

ANDREW turns upstage and faces ANTHONY. The two men look at one another.

PART THREE

Intervention

ANTHONY

The use of all this language and this positionality implicates Jamaicans in a certain way as being ignorant and insensitive and, for lack of a better word, homophobic, which I think even that, in a sense, is a simplification of it. Um. (5)

There is a difference between these two injustices, homophobia and racism, and they show up differently in the world. You know, often gay men will enjoy positions of economic and political power (1) that elude many Black men. And thereby my ability to fight that which is an injustice in my life... is diminished. It's not the same as your ability to fight it. (1) And I have, you know, friends of mine – for example I will post a picture of a Black man walking his child to school on Facebook and that will maybe get five people saying, "Hey, that's kind of cool." Um, but recently there was a photo of an African man walking in rural Africa with the multicoloured flag of the community, the rainbow flag, and thousands and thousands and thousands and thousands of people have praised this image. And that speaks to me about a certain disparity that nobody's looking at. And nobody fucking wants to. (2) Right? But my friend who I love dearly told me recently, there's this awakening happening in Africa. They're awakening to the right for Black men to be gay and how wonderful is that. I'm like, "Have you all awakened to the fact that for four hundred plus years that land was raped of its most precious resource – and those people created the economic infrastructure that you now live in? Has anyone awakened to that?" No. So. I have issues. Because there is hardly any context in which I as a Black man am free to stand up, either theatrically or publicly and say, "You know what? Your government policies? Your economic policies? Your social policies? (1) They're Murder Policies. They're murdering the hopes and lives of countless generations of Black men every day. And if you walk into any prison, you will see that."

> *ACTOR 5, who has been playing **ANTHONY**, holds for a beat and then descends from his elevated scaffolding platform. For the first time, **ANDREW** and another actor find themselves on the same level.*
>
> *The following speeches come from characters still remaining on the elevated scaffolding platforms. But now they are looking at **ANDREW** as they speak.*

JAMES
Now there's a whole lot of progressive, you know, white, you know, educated people going, you know, "The world can be a better place, a different place." And then wondering why everyone else is taking, like, why people are lagging behind. (2) Why people in these sort of, these lower-income brackets or these small countries, just don't *get with it*. (1) Well it took you *years* to, to brainwash communities into believing what you believed. Now you've changed your belief and you're wondering why we haven't changed ours yet?! It took time for you to brainwash us, and now it's going to take time to unbrainwash. It's a whole – I get really – I wish that people, recognize their – (2) how, how, they're implicated in it. (2) Right? As opposed to – (3)

They say some funny shit about arsonists. So (1) the typical MO for arsonists, the profile for arsonists, is one of two things. One of them, obviously, they love to set fires. But the, the fuckery about arsonists is that they'll return to the scene of the fire and – take on the hero role, too. So they tend to be the first person to talk to the media, uh, the first person to pull somebody out of the building, like, (*inhaling*) that's the MO – that arsonists will always return to the scene of the crime and often to take on the role of, um, um, (4) *saviour.*

That seems to be the profile for dominant communities in our culture. It's that they set the fire and then they return to put it out and then they ask for a medal.

JACQUELINE
What exactly are you going to do with these stories? You're speaking to Jamaicans, you're speaking to Canadians of Jamaican descent. But you realize it's not all one thing, right? There are connections to be made, but there's a lot that's different too.

JAMES
Now I'm not saying that, that, um, it's the fault of, like – I don't, I don't think white people should be more, "Oh my God, I'm an oppressor," like, I think that's self-defeating, like, who cares – like, I'm – like, I don't need, um, your guilt, like, that doesn't – I don't, I don't need that, right? But I do, and I would like your recognition of how you're not separate from the issue. Like, *you* – there's some connection to you and this issue. (2) Um. (1)

And then some people, (*wimpishly*) "I know oppression! Oh, you know, my family came from Ukraine, we were really poor and we ate turnips. And things like that." Yes. But you moved to a country (1) where (1) at some point in 1940, they decided that you weren't an *other* anymore and that, that you could join the club, as a white person, right? There was a time where, where, you know, um, (1) Eastern Europeans weren't considered, um, (1) *on par* with, with other white people, but there was a, there was a point in time, where someone said – you were let in, right? (1) Same thing happened to the Italians, same – there was a point where, someone decided, "Guess what! Welcome to the White Club!" And once you were given entrance to the club, *you used the pool.* (3) So own that *you used the pool.*

53

I recognize and understand that your great-grandmother ate turnips, you didn't build the pool. But you *used the pool*. You used the pool. (1) You're using the pool.

MICHAEL

You know, unfortunately, some of us who come out of the Black community, we're valued for what people think our equipments are, and we never have the conversation, "What is it, what is it like to be Black and gay in Canada? What does it mean to be gay within the context of your country of origin?" So, as you know, there are similarities and there are huge differences. Right? Because not everybody – I mean you can hide your sexuality, (1) I can hide my sexuality, (1) but I can't hide my colour. And so there are issues...

LEE

I think there's a new layer we have to unpackage, and this is the thing that has to happen now, is not – we don't have to focus on Brown people or people of colour, we have to focus on white people.

JACQUELINE

Your minority status as a gay guy is invisible. So you gotta own how you show up in the room. What we see is a white man, okay? And that gives you a certain amount of power. And what's disturbing or problematic is when you hang on to that power. When you define the experience. You hold the microphone. You approach people, to speak with them. That's exerting your power. You organizing their words in an order and sequence you see fit, that's exerting your power. That you're able to bring an audience together and have them engage with a subject matter of your choosing, that is your power. That you have support and funding, that is your power. And in this polarizing work, it is you who will be approached and told, "You are so brave. And you are doing such a good thing." And that is your power.

So what exactly are you going to do with these stories? They going to add to your power?

There's a saying, "The axe entered the forest and the trees looked to one another and said, 'Look, the *handle* is one of us.'" To me, the saying is about generosity. And how generosity can sometimes equip your enemies with what they need to take you down. Do you know what to do with these stories generously entrusted to you? Or will you hurt the very people you're trying to help?

> *Beat.* Then **ACTOR 1**, *who has been playing* **JACQUELINE**, *starts descending from her elevated scaffolding platform.* **ACTORS** *2, 3, and 4 do the same.* **ACTORS** *1–5 now all stand on the stage level and look at* **ANDREW**.

> **ANDREW** *turns back out to the audience and addresses his imagined friend.*

ANDREW
Someone said to me, "You should know, this investigation of yours, when I hear the stories you're focusing on – they really hurt me. Do they hurt you? Do they cost you something to listen to them? Because if they hurt me more than they hurt you, I'm not sure that you're the one who should be telling these stories."

And then someone else said, "Just tell the truth. If a story needs to be told... use your privilege, you know, to tell it."

Someone said to me, "This is going to turn out to be just another White Knight story: 'Well-meaning white guy investigates the barbarity of Black people. He shows them how they're not being good to each other and maybe, just maybe, they'll change.' It's *Dangerous Minds*. And you're Michelle Pfeiffer."

That same person said, "No one is going to tell you the truth. The real truth. No one is going to show you their Black pain. Because you don't deserve to see it. You can't be trusted to understand what it means."

And they said, "Why do we have to keep seeing white people discover Black suffering? Why is that the only way we get to hear our own stories?"

Someone said, "The situation for gay people in Ukraine is pretty shitty. Why don't you focus on that story?"

Someone said, "How do you leave Jamaica better than you found her? Is that possible?"

Someone said, "People are trained to admire power. You have power. And that's why no one will confront you on this."

Someone said, "White people get to tell whatever story they want. And what's worse, is that they'll be believed."

And then someone said, "You can't change who you are. But you can try and change the conversation." (2)

What's the conversation I want to be having? What am I doing, exactly?

Beat.

Did I think I was being a good friend? (1) Did I think I was helping you out? (1) When I said, "That's my story, too," did I think you'd feel relieved or less alone or something? (2) Did I assume you were feeling alone? Were you feeling alone? Or were you okay? (3) Was I feeling alone? (2) Did you feel like I took your story away from you? (1) Is that what I do? Take people's stories?

I am white.
I am male.
I was born in Canada.
I identify as Ukrainian Canadian.
We are both gay.
We are friends.

A Canadian guy loves his wife so much – her name is Wendy. And he decides he loves her so much that, as an act of devotion, he's gonna get her name tattooed on his dick. W-E-N-D-Y. But when he's soft, all you can make out is W-Y. So him and his wife take a trip to Jamaica and he finds himself at this urinal, standing next to this Jamaican dude. And he looks down and sees the very same W-Y on this Jamaican guy's junk. And out of excitement, this Canadian says, "Hey! Your tattoo – does it say 'WENDY'?" and the Jamaican guy says, "No man. No. (2) No. And why do you presume to know what's written on my dick?"

And when I tell that joke, every time, why do I picture the Jamaican as a Black man and the Canadian as a white man? Do you do the same? (2) Does that mean something?

> *ANDREW turns, looks back at the ACTORS 1–5, then turns out to the audience.*

ANDREW
My background, it sort of has multiple stages but first stage is Ukrainian, (1) uh, (1) is a Ukrainian upbringing in Montréal (?). Uh, (1) and going to Ukrainian school every Saturday and learning the language and Ukrainian dancing and doing Ukrainian Christmas and Easter. Um, speaking Ukrainian with grandparents and going to, uh, CYM (*pronounced "soom"*), which is a camp,

which was all Ukrainian kids, um, (1) CYM, (2) it's like a youth, (1) youth organization, (1) like a Ukrainian youth organization. (*inhale*) And so you would do these CYM camps every summer and you'd be in uniform and it was actually very militaristic: if you saw images of it, you would think, "Those kids are being trained to become an army, (2) uh, to go back to Ukraine, and (1) snatch the Homeland from the Soviets," like... yeah. Pretty bizarre.

And I was in that context till the age of eleven and had friends in that thoroughly Ukrainian environment and not really having many friends as a kid in my regular, sort of (1) regular life in Montréal. Um, (1) uh, going to church. Catholic (1) church. Um, (1) and then moving to Winnipeg at eleven, which is kind of the next phase and the, the Ukrainian aspect sort of dwindled then a little bit, but um – and that sort of gave over to, (1) uh, the all-boy, Jesuit education I got. Um, and that was, again, Catholic. Uh, and then into my adulthood, uh, sort of a shedding of church and I'd say the next phase was my sort of having my awakening as a gay person and realizing I was gay at nineteen and discovering that. Um, and that sort of being the next sort of phase of my background, which brings us to now, pretty well. Being gay. And being an artist. (3)

We were talking about the Jamaican Canadian community and Jamaican community and, uh, how you've visited Jamaica and you've felt really unsafe and how you've had, uh – certain family members have started treating you badly because (1) of who you are and, and because word has spread that you're gay (*inhale*) and I kind of went, "I hear ya man, I totally know what you're talking about – this is really familiar to me as a Ukrainian," (*inhale*) and uh, and then we just started talking about causes: religion, machismo, all these things that seemed like links between Ukrainians and Jamaicans, (*inhale*) and I zipped, I zipped to this idea that gay Ukrainians and gay Jamaicans had been split at birth or something. That my story and your story were the same story. Fundamentally. That something happening in your life was happening to me. But that's not what you were feeling. (1) You had your story. I had mine. (1) What lives in between stories? (2) Can you connect, without connecting stories?

> *A sudden shift. Electronic dance music. We are transported to Pride Toronto's street festivities, the morning before the parade. ACTORS 1–5 rotate through a series of voices. ANDREW leaps about, trying to catch them on his microphone.*

ANDREW
Because this is purely anonymous, can you all come up with a, a pseudonym, or a code name, or –

GAL 1
Old Man Jules.

GUY 1
Old Man Jules.

GAL 1 and GUY 1
Old Man Jules.

GUY 2
Degenerate.

ANDREW
Degenerate.

GUY 3
Ecstasy.

ANDREW
Ecstasy. You guys want in on this? We're doing an anonymous /

GUY 1
(*bratty laugh, then pointing successively at* **GUY 2, GAL 1,** *and* **GUY 3**) Her name is Kennedy. Her name is Colleen. And that's ... Bust-A-Nut. (*laughing*)

ANDREW
Bust-A-Nut. Awesome. Perfect Pride names.

COLLEEN
Do we want in on what?

ANDREW
I'm actually interviewing people around Pride about homophobia and racism in the city –

KENNEDY
Okay, wicked cool.

ANDREW
It's perfectly anonymous /

COLLEEN
Cool.

ANDREW
– and want to hear your opinions about this. Uh, in your opinion, what is the most homophobic or one of the worst places on Earth for a gay or queer person.

GUY 1
London, Ontario. (*laughing*)

> **ALL** laugh "No." The **ACTORS** morph into a new, even more rapid-fire sequence of revellers.

CW
Oh God, loads of places in Africa, for starters.

BLAZE
Israel.

JOHNNIE B
Jamaica.

ANDREW
Why do you say Jamaica?

JOHNNIE B
Y'know, I've heard a lot of stories...

ANDREW
Specifically.

JOHNNIE B
Uh, (1) I'm trying to think of one actually /

DINGER
All kinds of places in Africa and Asia and the Middle East. Uh /

CW
On earth!?!

DINGER
I've spoken to a couple people from Jamaica /

BLACK MAMBO
Our friend Jordan.

DINGER
– and uh, the, they, they justify murdering people just because they're gay.

JOHNNIE B
Oh yah, our friend Jordan is from Jamaica /

BLACK MAMBO
Yah like, he, like –

JOHNNIE B
His mom would shoot him if he came / out.

JASMINE
Middle /

BLAZE
Middle East.

JASMINE
Middle East, I think.

CALLY
The States? For one. They can be harsh.

JANATHA
I think Poland.

TOBY
That... (*hesitantly*) Cam-e-roon? I don't / know what it is.

GEORGE
Uh, maybe Africa and the Middle East.

STEVE
High sch/ooooool.

DJ
Uganda.

CW
Jamaica.

ANDREW
Why?

EMC
I don't know, I just know that there's a lot of homophobia there.

ANDREW
Okay. And do you think we have any responsibility to those countries, to those struggling communities?

CW
Oh yes, we do.

DINGER
Yes. Yes, we do.

BILL
No.

TYRONE
Well yah –

SILVIA
I do! Yah.

ANDREW
What can we do?

CW
Well it's going to take bloodshed. (*laughing*) (2)

ANDREW
Yeah?

CW
Well, it's, it's gonna have to take a bit of confrontation.

SEXY SILL
Give 'em a good swift kick, a good swift kick in the ass, yeah.

> *ACTORS 2, 3, and 5 drop their characters, leave the stage, and sit in the audience. ANDREW is left onstage with two women, COCOA and SUNSHINE.*

ANDREW
I'm gonna give you five minutes! So I wanted to ask you to give yourselves code names because this is anonymous.

SUNSHINE
Right.

ANDREW
So what code name would you want / or nickname?

SUNSHINE
Sunshine.

ANDREW
Sunshine? (2)

COCOA
Well, um … Cocoa.

ANDREW
Cocoa. I'd love to know what you think, in your opinion, what is
the worst place on the planet for gay people or queer people? (2)
You can list a number of places if it's more than one. (5)

*COCOA pushes ANDREW's microphone aside. For the remainder of
the scene, ANDREW holds it down by his side.*

COCOA
You know what? I don't like answerin' that question.

ANDREW
Wh–

COCOA
Why? Because I don't think, I don't think it's that simple (?). Like,
I think it's pretty shitty here in Toronto. Same way shitty in, like,
a so-called Third World country (?). But I think in a so-called
Third World country, I mean, like, the West here puts stuff
in place.

ANDREW
Yeah.

COCOA
Right, but makes it really horrible for LGBT people in those
countries, so –

ANDREW
Talk about that.

COCOA
That, I can't...

COCOA gestures that she can't get into it: too big.

ANDREW
Talk about –

COCOA
Well, I mean, it's, um, the US, um, churches that go down to, say, a place like Uganda and telling them that they needed to criminalize homosexuality and kill them /

ANDREW
Yeah /

COCOA
Right? And actually givin' money to the government to make sure that's enforced. So hey! You know, like, so, so, I have a really hard time /

ANDREW
Yeah /

COCOA
Talkin' about that. I, I can't give you a country.

ANDREW
Yeah.

COCOA
No.

SUNSHINE
For me, you can't talk about homophobia without – talk about
homophobia in colonized places without talking about the history
of colonization /

COCOA
Yah /

SUNSHINE
And the impact that was put on, like, enslaved people to
reproduce /

COCOA
Yah.

ANDREW
Yeah.

SUNSHINE
And that kind of thing for hundreds of years and then Western
countries turn around after making, after building things on
the backs of people of colour and then want to say, "You're
homophobic" /

COCOA
Yah /

SUNSHINE
"You're horrible and we're the perfect ones." So I have /

COCOA
I can't /

SUNSHINE
Yeah.

ANDREW
Do you think most people on Church Street here... have that in mind in any way, shape, or / form?

COCOA
No /

ANDREW
An awareness that colonialism has something to do / with –

COCOA
No, no, not / really.

SUNSHINE
No, I don't think so.

COCOA
I mean, there's a good bit of us. (*looking over ANDREW's shoulder, down Church Street*) There's a good bit of us but not, no, this crowd today, / no.

ANDREW
Do you think it's important that they know something like that?

COCOA
Of course!

SUNSHINE
I do, I mean if I was walking past the global human rights thing down there and seeing, um, like, all the information, the stats as, "Oh in Iran, oh in Uganda" /

COCOA
Yah /

SUNSHINE
"Oh, in this place. Oh, in all these places with colonization," but
they're forgettin', "Oh in Canada, still beatings happen from t–"

COCOA
And stupid little Pride, you know, like, (1) "Oh, are you really gay?
We don't want you in here." You know, like, "You, you cause fights"
or "No, we don't want a Black Night in the club here because you
guys don't spend enough money at the bar" or – so I mean…

ANDREW
So, do you feel, I'd love to ask, which do you think is a more
burning issue in the city: homophobia or racism?

SUNSHINE
I don't think either is more burning /

COCOA
Yah /

SUNSHINE
I don't think racism is going to end without homophobia ending.
I don't think /

COCOA
Yah /

SUNSHINE
We'll ever get anywhere without racism / ending.

ANDREW
Right.

COCOA
But we have to talk about, we, we have to – the *intersectionality* of it all.

ANDREW
So you think the intersection is key if w–

COCOA
Yep.

ANDREW
If we'–

COCOA
Yes.

ANDREW
– we're more aware of that inter/section –

COCOA
Yes!

ANDREW
– would we become / better?

COCOA
Well yeah, but I think people need – with that, though, you need to recognize your place in that and how you perpetuate that /

ANDREW
Yep.

COCOA
And, you know, let go of some of your shit.

ANDREW
Yeah.

COCOA
And move on. But that's the problem, letting go, so now, you *see* people who are of so-called knowledge not – letting – go /

ANDREW
Yeah /

COCOA
– of that power, right? So –

ANDREW
Can you speak to me about what I may be hanging onto, unknow/ingly?

COCOA
I don't know! I don't know where / you're at!

ANDREW
I know –

COCOA
I mean you're asking us questions and we're going at it. So I'm, I'm thinking that probably you've been thinking about things, / so –

ANDREW
I've been thinking about the exact things you've been talking about /

COCOA
Yah /

ANDREW
Can I ask what your home is or what you identify as home?

COCOA
I'm from Trinidad and Tobago.

ANDREW
Trinidad and Tobago.

COCOA
And actually it's Pride weekend there right now.

ANDREW
Okay.

COCOA
Yep! They don't – we don't have a march or anything but certainly we have, like – we have clubs. Yup. Regular. And we have clubs an' we have groups that, you know, that, who are doing amazin' work and not only in Trinidad but, um, other parts of the Caribbean and make connections actually with the West, right?

ANDREW
Great.

COCOA
So we're one of the countries that's *really* working, really, really hard, you know, / so –

ANDREW
'Cause a lot of people mention Jamaica when I ask that first question /

COCOA
Yah /

ANDREW

Jamaica was the first place they mention.

COCOA

Yah. (2) And you know what? I can't – That is just *pure fucking racism*. I can't take it. I'm not saying stuff is not happening there, / but no.

SUNSHINE

People think that you can't live there, but there are many people who are out / enjoying and living out –

COCOA

Bullshit! And well! And they don't want to come here!

SUNSHINE

And like, it's a complicated relationship / with, yeah, it's complicated histories –

COCOA

Yah. Yep, yep, it is, but um, yeah, *no*. It's a *shame* that they say that and, and then with that kind of message, then you're having people from Jamaica even wanting to believe it so my thing is that I'm not, I, I'm – I have to ensure my – 'cause I'm a lesbian, I want to ensure that *my* people know that this is bullshit – this um, Western mentality, that we are so vicious and –

SUNSHINE

And at the same time, it's so important to note that, um, we have had different experiences and I'm not trying to say that people don't have violent experiences /

COCOA

Of course! /

SUNSHINE
– that people don't feel unsafe at home but the kind of unsafety, um, that a lot of my queer friends of colour feel in the mainstream queer space of Toronto is jus', is like, ridiculous too /

COCOA
Yes! /

SUNSHINE
And like, the exotification that takes place /

COCOA
Oh it's gross! I've been called n***** on this strip how many times.

ANDREW
Really.

COCOA
Of course!

COCOA's voice has gone high in pitch.

ANDREW
By, by white people?

COCOA
Of course.

ANDREW
By not-white people?

COCOA
White.

ANDREW
Why, why would somebody, why would somebody – ih –

SUNSHINE
Be/cause –

COCOA
Because that's the place you will go with me.

SUNSHINE
Mm. And then, also like, um, because people assume that, like, Blackness, Black equals homophobic /

COCOA
Yes! /

SUNSHINE
It's kind of thing, like, you're here, like, you don't belong here. So /

COCOA
Yah-yah-yah-yah-yah /

SUNSHINE
Your people can't be here so you're…

COCOA
Yah.

ANDREW
Um. One last, last question /

COCOA
Yah /

ANDREW

If you had a message, question, or request to put to intolerant people – whether it be the intolerant person who, uh, (1) offends you on this strip or the city at large – what is your message, / question –

COCOA

Well okay! I don't want anyone to tolerate me so there, so *I'm done!* I don't want a – I – don't tolerate me. I *hate* that /

ANDREW

Yeah /

COCOA

I don't wanna / be tolerated –

ANDREW

It's not good enough.

COCOA

Eh – no – it's not *good*. I don't want to be tolerated. Oh my God I need for you to see *me* and, and *all* the complexities that come with it. Don't tolerate my ass.

ANDREW

So how do we change? How do we become more –

SUNSHINE

Work on your own sh/it –

COCOA

Shit. Yeeeeaaaahhh!

SUNSHINE

Work on your own / shit.

COCOA
Work on your own shit.

*ACTORS 1 and 2, who have played **COCOA** and*
***SUNSHINE**, walk past **ANDREW** and sit with the*
*audience. **ANDREW** is left alone onstage.*

PART FOUR

Work on Your Own Shit

*At first almost imperceptibly, **ANDREW** repeats the phrase "Work on your own shit." It is a riddle. And a mantra. He tries it on the microphone, but he quickly rejects the amplification of his voice. He places the microphone on the empty chair that remains in the middle of the space.*

ANDREW
Work on your own shit.
Work on your own shit.
Work on your own shit.
Work on your own shit.
Work on your own shit.

He repeats the phrase. He speaks it at first from a standstill, unsure of what it actually means. As he repeats the phrase, he begins to move. What starts as a walk turns into a run around the space.

Work on your own shit.
Work on your own shit.
Work on your own shit.
Work on your own shit.
Work on your own shit.

Eventually he starts removing the sandbags that stabilize the base of the scaffolding structure – revealing casters. At first, he carries these sandbags into the centre of the space, then throws them like shot puts, from a distance.

*His pace accelerates. His voice grows louder, his breath
more laboured.*

*Once the sandbags have been removed, he proceeds to
unlock all the casters at the base of the scaffolding. To do
so, he has to stomp down onto a locking mechanism with
his heel, making the whole structure shake with each
unlocking.*

Work on your own shit!
Work on your own shit!
Work on your own shit!
Work on your own shit!
Work on your own shit!

*Once all the casters are unlocked, he attempts to move
the entire scaffolding structure, all the while repeating
the phrase. He is hardly successful with moving the
massive structure. It shifts crookedly by no more than
a metre before **ANDREW** collapses with unfeigned
exhaustion.*

*From the audience, **MICHAEL** approaches **ANDREW**,
who remains on the ground, out of breath.*

MICHAEL
(*to ANDREW*) How do you actually talk, in the Jamaican context,
with the issue that's going on in the Jamaican context. And, and
there's a whole bunch of things that are going – at play. There's
always been an intolerance in the Jamaican context around
homosexuality. It's *increasingly* violent. But there are a whole host
of things around the violence, right?

And you've got to unpack it to know what's the strategy. 'Cause
maybe the strategy you're using is not the appropriate strategy,

'cause it's not contextual and it's not attentive to the complexity of what's actually happening on the ground. The discourse has to change. You can't have a North American conversation around these things. (3)

I want to hear your story. I want to hear what has shaped you. I mean, your role, as a person of power and privilege in terms of whiteness, is to make sure that, um, somehow those stories get heard – ha! – by others and somehow that people understand the complexity of human relationships and that kind of stuff, right? And it's not something you do alone. It's something that you do in partnership with others. Whatever you do, don't simplify it. Because it's a complex, complex, complex issue. Once you simplify it, you... You may never get to the nub of it. But there is something in the trying.

And that's your task. And the dilemma for you: Are you prepared for your own personal transformation? (*laughing*)

After a long beat, **ANDREW** *starts this speech from his prostrate position on the ground. He is still out of breath.*

ANDREW
My background, it sort of has multiple stages but first stage is Ukrainian, (1) uh, (1) is a Ukrainian upbringing in Montréal (?). Uh, (1) and going to Ukrainian school every Saturday and learning the language and Ukrainian dancing and doing Ukrainian Christmas and Easter. Um, speaking Ukrainian with grandparents and going to, uh, CYM (*pronounced "soom"*) which is a camp, which was all Ukrainian kids, um, (1) CYM, (2) it's like a youth, (1) youth organization, (1) like a Ukrainian youth organization. (*inhale*) And so you would do these CYM camps every summer and you'd be in uniform and it was actually very militaristic: if you saw images of it, you would think, "Those kids are being trained to become an army, (2) uh, to go back to Ukraine, and (1) snatch the Homeland from the Soviets," like... yeah. (1) Given the recent shit

that's been going down in Ukraine, uh, those images of us as kids flash through my brain a bit more frequently. This idea that we were some kind of (1) group of saviours that could be called on at any moment to ... take Russia on.

ANDREW gets up and begins delivering the rest of this biography to audience members, including ACTORS 1–5.

We moved in 1991 to Winnipeg. My dad worked for the railroad and so we moved from that thoroughly Ukrainian community in Montréal to the Prairies. Which I would say is the next phase of my background. Um, (1) I'd say I was a pretty religious kid to begin with and that was only more pronounced in my early adolescence. Yeah. Catholic. My parents weren't very religious. Just me, for some reason. I remember I came up with this idea – I used to take two strips of masking tape and tape these little crosses on my books, on my nightstand, and above my light switch in my room, and on my full-length mirror. I put them there to remind me to be good. Um, (1) I was called a faggot throughout all of junior high. It never occurred to me that I was one. Girls liked me a lot. I always got along well with girls and was always dating someone. I wasn't manly. But I was nice. (1) Christina, Natasha, Kim, Charlene, Rachel, Pam, Robynne. (1) Starting in grade nine, I went to an all-boy, Jesuit high school. Um, and that was, again, Catholic. I think my single biggest takeaway from Jesuit high school was, is (2) this idea of stewardship, which um, I think has, you know, is essentially about looking after things. The definition I recall from my teachers was, um, that it's our responsibility to leave the world better than we found it. And um, I think that's something I've become obsessed with, that idea, with, um (?) ... Uh, my family moved to Alberta. And I entered my adulthood, uh, with a sort of shedding of church, stopped praying, took the masking tape down, stopped believing, and I'd say the next phase was my sort of having my awakening as a gay person, and realizing

81

I was gay at nineteen and discovering that. Um, (1) I didn't come out to my family as I had planned. I came out to my mother on the Deerfoot Highway in Calgary. She had – she was driving me to the airport because I was taking a trip with some friends. Moments earlier I had said goodbye to my then boyfriend – she had no idea that he was my boyfriend – but I was giving him a hug goodbye in our entryway – he had popped by to wish me a good trip – I gave him a hug and my mother came around the corner and, uh, and I sent him off. And as soon as I closed the door on him, my mother said, "What is going on? Boys don't hug like that." I had a flight to catch, so we hopped into the Jeep Cherokee and we had this (1) conversation hurtling down the Deerfoot at 130 kilometres an hour. And I could barely focus, I could barely focus because all I could think was that in all these books I'd been reading on how to come out to your parents, in every single book it said, "Under no circumstances should you ever, *ever* come out to a parent who is driving a vehicle." And so there I am, the whole time thinking, "We are going to die. We are going to die. Jeeps can flip over easily, right? And so my worked-up mother is going to flip this Jeep and my gayness will be to blame." (2) That didn't happen. (2)

ANDREW looks to his fellow ACTORS who have been seated in the audience, then to MICHAEL. ANDREW makes his way to a new position onstage.

PART FIVE

Trying to Listen Differently

ANDREW

(*to the audience*) In the summer of 2011, during Pride, a Jamaican
dancehall music artist named Capleton came to Toronto. He is
known for some violently anti-gay lyrics and was forced to move
his concert from the downtown to Brampton following criticism
from the gay community. Not all of his songs contain homophobic
lyrics, but there are references in some of them to acts like "Bun
out ah chi chi, / Blood out ah chi chi," referring to burning and
bleeding a homosexual. His management team was claiming
that these were songs that he *used* to sing and that he hadn't
performed them in years. During the whole ordeal, the media
couldn't reach his team for comment. My director Alan and I had
better luck. We spoke with his manager. I wasn't going to include
her voice originally because I wasn't sure of how to give it space.
I reconsidered. I want to see if I can try and listen differently.

> *CLAUDETTE starts to speak from the audience,*
> *then eventually gets onstage and faces ANDREW.*
> *ANDREW faces her.*

CLAUDETTE

Time heals. And time takes care of everything. Because Capleton is
a very (3) peace– peaceful man. (1) Contrary to what they might
make it look like. So we just need to take time, time take – time
take care of everything, ya man. (1) And they don't understand
how Jah's mind works. Because He works in a mysterious way.

And that policeman who came, (1) let me say that racism has
reared its ugly head in the form of homosexuality and free…

dom of choice. In the meantime that we are fighting for freedom of our rights, we practising racism, and they going back to black and white. (1) In our, our culture – which I'm so proud to be a Jamaican – and here it is, that someone is in their culture, and they're singing based on what is presented *to them*. (1) Not what they know – and if I tell you something you don't believe me, that we're all suffering from culture shock. (1) When we knew that homosexuality was something that was practised by all these people we personally look up to, because in our culture we're taught that white people are the, the gods of the world (2) because we're coming from slavery, (1) so we see white man can go out there and behave just like any other ordinary man, it shock us! We are descendants of slavery – you know that, right? You know our culture? White plantation owners used to rape the Black men in front of their wives. (4) That is why, that is part of the genesis of the resentment. In Jamaica, why they sing all these songs all the time, sing about these pedophiles, sing about the rapists, and they sing about these men. (2) So (1) when they talk about burn somebody – when they say "bun the fire" – it's a *metaphor*. Bun fire, bun dem. Fire bun.

They have taken something from a cultural basis to an international basis, (1) an' now it becomes lack of freedom for someone else. We are no longer free in the world. That's what took place in Toronto. (3) It was just one group of people who got to the police, said, "You come here and you should not be here during gay pride week," we, we in Jamaica don't know anything about gay pride week, we comin' there, we don't know nuttin'. (2) And it's not fair. (1) We don't know anything about gay pride week. That's your pride. You be free to do whatever you do. Whatever you think your rights. Hm? (1) Whatever you do. Every man (1) has the right to do what he wants to do. (2)

Maybe you should come to Jamaica. Find me and I will take you around. You would see what's happening here. (2)

ANDREW

And if I were to come down there, and you would show me what's happening, I would be safe?

CLAUDETTE

Of course. Of course. (3) We're not barbarians.

ANDREW

I know.

CLAUDETTE

I don't ask people if they're gay – who they are – I don't care – that's their business. That's your right, who you want to be.

ANDREW

(*to the audience again*) I first approached my friend, Narnia – or Annabel as she called herself, to initiate me. I wanted to hear about her Jamaican background, to give me some lay of the land, to help me navigate this subject matter. It was an immensely generous act, for her to sit with me, to answer my questions. Even my insensitive ones. When I listen, really listen back to our earliest conversation, there are so many things that I missed.

> As with **CLAUDETTE, ANNABEL** starts in the
> audience and then makes it onstage, dialoguing
> with **ANDREW.**

ANNABEL

Slavery... man... slavery is... I... the one, one of the things that I think as human beings is most important to us is... being seen and validated, and slavery – works – to – eradicate that, from a person's existence. And you have to find all kinds of ways to do that, right? All kinds of insidiyous, um, insidious, um, systematic ways of making sure, eradicating a person's culture, their language, their practices, not giving them combs so that they can take care of their hair, um… taking babies from their mothers, um… um, um, um, telling them that they're ugly… um, w– women not being in ownership of their own bodies, so, you know, you can come in and have sex anytime… and, I don't see why it'd've been any different for men. I don't see why it would have been any different for men. (4)

(*inhaling*) I meet so many people… I love – one of the reasons why I *love* the fact that I, I built a life in Canada is because it's like the world has come to me. Right? Um… you know, I, I can take the streetcar and go to another country. I can take a *train* and *really* go to another country if I'm going to Montréal, if I'm willing to pay. Um (*inhaling*). Ah… and, you know, and you choose the people who you want to have be a part of your life because there are things that, that they add to your life, that you have deemed valuable… and when those people are a mixture of races and backgrounds… then sometimes, the sense is that we're *all the same*… and, the way slavery has marked me… is, me – *this person* – I'm not saying it's this way for anybody else – *this person* knows that we're not.

ANDREW
(*to the audience*) I interviewed Gareth Henry in my downtown apartment, at my kitchen table. I wanted to hear about his activism with J-FLAG, the Jamaica Forum for Lesbians, All-Sexuals, and Gays. I wanted to hear about his friend Brian Williamson. Brian was a white Canadian who had helped found J-FLAG and in 2004 was murdered, stabbed dozens and dozens of times with a knife. I wanted to hear about what happened to Gareth on Valentine's Day 2007, how he got trapped in a pharmacy inside a Kingston mall, a mob of several hundred people outside calling out for him and two other gay men. I wanted to hear about the violence and the threat of violence that his friends still contend with. He ended up telling me these stories. I found myself at my kitchen table, crying with him. I felt that his story was my story. His injustice was

my injustice. I wanted to do something about it. But I think I was so focused on the doing part that I missed some of the seeing part.

> GARETH *emerges from the audience. He walks over to the "listening chair" centre stage. He picks up the microphone that ANDREW had abandoned during the "Work on Your Own Shit" sequence. He sits in the chair and speaks into the microphone.*

GARETH
(*inhaling*) In the four and half years that I was involved, actively involved with J-FLAG, thirteen of my friends were killed. And thirteen (*his voice going up*) is a lot people. You know, to lose one person is so hard. An' it's a great loss. But to do, to do that, go through that process thirteen different times, you know, it's (*tsk-tsking a few times*), it's not easy.

I remember Victor Jarett, he was beaten by police and then turned over to a mob.

I remember Steve, he was shot in the head – Steve was my co-worker. I had to go identify his body and the police called me faggot, battyman while I did it.

This is happening. So what do we do?

ANDREW
James, the pastor, said to me: ...

> *Lastly, JAMES emerges from the audience.*

JAMES
Everyone desires connection. We all desire connection. So now what if we could get people to a place where we can find ways that *everyone* – that people can begin to connect with others in *real*,

uh ... uh, meaningful ways that don't require someone else being, um, objectified or diminished or scapegoated or *othered*. What if we connected in that way?

By now, ACTORS 1–5 and ANDREW find themselves in the bestrewn space: a pile of sandbags, the chair, the partially dislocated scaffolding structure.

They look at one another for a long while.

Then, in their own time, ACTORS 1–5 walk over to the bases of their respective platforms and scale the scaffolding. They resume their original positions on their platforms, though now at different angles, given the shifting of the structure. They look out at the audience.

ANDREW turns back to the audience; he is with his imagined friend, again.

ANDREW
You are Black.
You are male.
You were born in Jamaica.
You identify as Jamaican Canadian.
We are both gay.
We are friends.
You told me a story once.
I thought it was our story.
I thought it was my story.

Someone said to me: (1) "You should hand over the keys. That might be the best way for us to take a white guy asking all these questions and sharing these stories, even his own story, if we saw him hand over the keys, give over the power."

My friend, I imagined handing you the keys.
I imagined creating a space for you to speak in.
To be heard.
To give you your story back.
To address your injustice, the injustice in your life.
Which is *different* than the injustice in my life.
That our injustices could meet and we wouldn't force them to be
the same, we would just listen, and let them be what they are.
I wanted the opportunity to do that with you because I didn't the
first time. My friend, I'm sorry for not listening well enough.
I want to try and listen differently.
To listen better.

*The lights come down, though for a moment linger on
the* **ACTORS** *atop their platforms.*

THE END

The Passing of the Mic

Following each performance of *Small Axe* in Toronto, the audience was invited to participate in something the production called the Passing of the Mic. After the bows and the exit of the performers, one of the staff members from the Black Coalition for AIDS Prevention (Black CAP) took the stage. This facilitator spoke to their lived experiences as a Black queer person navigating the intersection of homophobia and racism. On numerous evenings, this was a person who shared aspects of their personal refugee journey. For a few minutes, they spoke on the wireless microphone that Andrew used in the performance. Following their words, the mic would be passed through the audience. Any audience member who had chosen to remain for this voluntary activity was invited to say something. The rest of the room was asked to listen without judgment. Some people spoke. Some people passed the mic.

This post-show offering was not attended or witnessed by Andrew in any way. It was not recorded or documented, either. The intention was to create a space that was not being moderated by a white person or a white presence, especially not the artist who had crafted the theatrical experience that had just taken place. The Passing of the Mic was intended as a kind of epilogue for the audience wherein people could utter their feelings, contemplate the themes and issues of the play, share their own stories, and, to the best of their ability, listen to one another.

Inside of Another House

A RECORDED ENCOUNTER BETWEEN
PLAYWRIGHTS ANDREW KUSHNIR AND
KHARI WENDELL McCLELLAND

On June 2021, collaborators Andrew Kushnir and Khari Wendell McClelland spoke for several hours about their work together, the possibilities of theatre, and this book you are reading. The following – a slightly truncated version of their conversation, verbatim – was always intended as the midpoint of this two-play anthology that is *Moving the Centre*. A dialogue between artists and friends. Some headings have been provided to identify the key movements and themes of their dialogue.

INSIDE OF ANOTHER HOUSE

KHARI WENDELL McCLELLAND: Well, it isn't tidy.

ANDREW KUSHNIR: *Small Axe.*

KWM: Right? As I finished reading it – and maybe this is what it was like for audiences – I thought, this isn't neat. This is still being figured out. You know, like, there's something about this that is still in its unfolding.

AK: Yes.

KWM: That some kind of iterative process is happening here. And I understood the challenge of it, the danger between reifying stereotypes, but also the danger of not surfacing certain things happening in the world. I kept reading and thinking, "This is hard." And after reading the play – because I didn't know you when it played to audiences and

I didn't see the show – I was left with this inner feeling of not being settled. Of being a little bit churned.

AK: It's interesting, because this book we're making is comprised of documentary plays. In that regard, the plays are a record of something that happened both on stage and in life. They are record, memory, and event, all combined. And *Small Axe*, as the work that precedes *Freedom Singer*, is useful information. There are echoes and connection points and some insight into how I, as a co-creator, was an unsettled collaborator of yours. I think it's always valuable to remember, with any artist, that any given project has a lifespan with the public – and that the artist, if they're inclined and able, keeps going on to something else, some new form of the question. Big questions or concerns or hopes cannot be capped. They migrate.

KWM: The complicated question I'm left with, and this is a bridge into *Freedom Singer*, is this idea of space. Making a space. A place to gather. And I think maybe *Small Axe* was the beginning of you trying to cultivate a kind of space where we don't have to be exactly the same, but can still be together, right? A space where we can care, support, love, witness each other? You know, people have their affinity groups, their tendency towards caucusing versus congressing. My impression is that you were trying to blur the edges, for yourself, for others. Yes, in part, to create a space to see, feel, identify, and experience the nature of oppression. And also the self-work, the smaller space to work through one's own complicated and often fraught encounter with the world. And trying to integrate those forms of understanding. And it's really complex, because sometimes that process unfolds with people similar to you, and then other times with people very different from you. There's a real tension there. That kind of learning can be a bumpy ride.

AK: I could not have undertaken *Small Axe* without the collaborators who came together around that work.

KWM: And still there are a lot of risks.

AK: Indeed. And it came at some cost to those artists. Some of the actors, for instance. I know that some of the actors of colour involved in the project were challenged by their peers: "Why are you working on that show?" The premise of the play is treacherous. It's in the doing, in the relational work of the play, that something else may be possible.

KWM: How do we set each other up for success? And "success," that's just another word for a sense of reciprocity inside of a space, where there is something genuine about the exchange. It's a space where I don't feel like I'm being bombarded or being patronized or talked down to or used or forced through something. A space where I can feel a deep sense of genuine curiosity and stay out of my judging mind. And again, this is not just for the audience, this is also for the players. It sounds to me like you fought for that space.

AK: I definitely felt that this was the work of the play and the practice of *Small Axe*. As a group of artists, we sought out that space, sometimes finding it, sometimes doubting it was possible. I think we kept reconsidering, How do we help everyone show up for the voices of the play? So that they're not just characters we can process through our personal vantage points, so that they're not consumable, but rather people we show up for.

KWM: It's challenging. You know with audiences, with artists even, some people are drawn to controversial subjects. Just because they like the crunchiness of it.

AK: The conflict.

KWM: That's right. But in a kind of cool, reserved way, where they're not actually affected by it. They just like seeing people kind of stirring, people in the state of drama or anguish. They get something from that.

AK: And they don't have to actually – there's no skin in the game, as it were.

KWM: I get that they bought a ticket. They gave their money. But it's kind of like that whole colonial thing, right? Like this idea of reparations. I feel that there are many people in this world, if they were told they could write a cheque, and that everything would be fine, they'd be super down for that.

AK: Yeah.

KWM: Like, that's the kind of reconciliation they want. They want to go: "Here. Here's the $1,356.88. I hope you feel good. Can we just carry on now?"

AK: Yeah.

KWM: What I get so interested in, through the art and the practice of sharing stories, is that we can do better than that transaction. You've got me thinking about that idea of "working on your own shit." Is there a terminal degree for your shit? Know what I'm saying? Is it pass or fail? Like, how do you know if you're doing or have done the work? Where's the line? Is there one?

AK: I don't think there's a line. Or if there is, I think it's a horizon one keeps moving towards.

KWM: And it's not a tidy journey, just like the issues that get surfaced in these plays.

AK: I see a lot of kinship between *Small Axe* and *Freedom Singer*, even though they're very different offerings.

KWM: There are definitely questions that carry over. I could see how you completed that process and may have still been thinking, "These questions could live inside of another house."

AK: How do we co-exist with difference? How do we actually challenge our human tendency to group and receive the particulars of someone? How do we discover commonality, mutuality at no one's expense? How do we embrace plurality as a strength of our communities, the spaces we occupy? And I suppose, how do we bring all of these questions into the theatre?

KWM: That sounds right.

AK: Why did you turn to theatre, do you think?

KWM: I was coming from a folk and roots music background. And the way, the way I was seeing work being presented, it just felt so boring to me, honestly. I was looking for some other way to tell the story of the music, but also the story of me, my family, how we find the songs.

AK: The songs your ancestral grandmother may have sung on her way to Canada, through the Underground Railroad.

KWM: That's right. But I sensed it was also a story about Canada, a story about history, how histories get shared, how stories live and die through song and otherwise. A story in a story.

AK: Right.

KWM: I thought, "I want to do something that compels people, that makes them ... *remember*. That makes them *feel*." And I was drawn to the pace of theatre. Music is fast and unrelenting. Things don't always get the time they need. And indeed, theatre turned out to be more methodical, as I'd hoped. Theatre can have this ritual to it, a practice of doing things over and over, reciting, saying it over and over with new audiences, and that's tougher to come by in the music world.

AK: My theory is that you have a real appetite for metaphor. For symbol. You weren't a theatre person by training, but the way in which everything is metaphor in the theatre, everything represents something beyond itself ... that spoke to you. I remember when we were trying to figure out the set design for *Freedom Singer*, you shared an image with me.

KWM: The philosopher's stone symbol.*

AK: And that became the basis of the set, two concentric circles and a square and a triangle. The mysticism of that geometry impacted the show.

KWM: That symbol represented something foundational for me. And at the time, amidst the struggle of searching for certain parts of my ancestry, I remember I was looking for foundational things. There's such a relational quality between the geometric shapes in this image. Circle as a shape for reducing hierarchy in terms of meeting spaces, meeting people. The triangle is this trinity, that sort of "when two or more are gathered, then there am I with them" kinda thing. And the

---

* Or "Squared Circle."

square, well, we can say, "That's really square!" but it's understood as being the Western structural imperative. But it's foundational to our buildings, to the even distribution of weight, and the capacity to climb upward. There's such a poem within that emblem.

AK: When you describe that, I feel the theatre in all of it. And I think it gives a window onto the kind of mysticism you were bringing into your storytelling and theatre-making. Do you remember the piece of cloth you brought into the rehearsal space? It had strawberries on it or something like that.

KWM: Yeah, yeah, it looked like hearts, it looked like strawberries. It looked like little flashes of fire, like microphones. It was an Aboriginal block print from Australia, and I was compelled by it. * It had energy for me. And it felt to me that through these things, what we were exploring was ceremony. It all felt more grounded. Rooted, but also ascendant. The performance and story find an anchor in that, but also it can shoot up more.

---

*   The fabric is the work of Daly River artist Kieren Karritpul – who also works in painting, printmaking, and ceramics. He is the youngest director ever appointed to the Association of Northern, Kimberley, and Arnhem Aboriginal Artists (ANKAAA).

AK: You're making me reflect on how we can intentionally make the theatre the site of ceremony. And how ceremonies matter. I think we even use the word "liturgy" when we – I don't know if that's too much of a Judeo-Christian concept – but what does it mean to undergo a script as liturgy every night with a different group of people in the audience?

KWM: Oh my gosh, I ... Look, it just came to me, I feel, like, emotional as I'm saying it, but I was just thinking about the recurring triangles in the design, and then me, Tanika Charles (who played the Chorus in *Freedom Singer*) and Noah Walker (who played the Guitarist) onstage, that triangular relationship, but also how ... how that liturgy I was performing was an incantation that brought forth a different kind of trinity in my life: a baby and a father ...

AK: You're referring to your biological dad that you recently reconnected with, and then your daughter, who was born in late 2020.

KWM: That's right.

AK: Life and art, all intertwined.

KWM: It makes me think of *Freedom Singer* on all these multiple layers. The piece was politics, it was prayer, a deep asking of the self, deep asking of the witness, the realm of Dream and Possibility, like an aspirational calling into reality. (*pause*) That's, like, hitting me. How personally profound the practice was. It felt like the act of ancestral veneration. Even though I was telling the story, *Freedom Singer* was very much about women in my life, supporting me, guiding me, and me in return holding and giving props to them. Raising my hands to them. Yeah, I feel very emotional, like, all of a sudden, it's ... (*pause*) One of the most powerful moments of the play for me is those last few lines in the script, "I just wish there was a place where we can all be together." I just wish there was a place where we could be together – and I mean that directly in relationship to my family, but I also think what that means for me about community, what that means for me about difference. There's an individual experience, there's the experience of those who you might feel a very close affinity to, but also I, for whatever reason, from a very young age, have really been excited and interested in people who are different than me.

AK: Right.

KWM: It seems to me that with *Small Axe*, you were working the same riddle – and maybe that's part of what brought us together. I keep recognizing in my work that I just want there to be a place where we can be together in a genuinely conversational space – a space of love, a space for food, space for worship and ritual, space for friendship, for life-making and romance, and a space for our children. I think one of the deepest leanings in my heart is to find a space where we can be emotionally honest and authentic and revealed, and where there's a sense of reciprocity.

CAN I SEE A LITTLE BIT OF THEIR EYES?!

AK: I think back to how much vulnerability you brought to our creation process – a new one to you – and then performances, too. Big sections of the *Freedom Singer* script are born of interviews I conducted with you, recorded encounters we had over the course of a few years. There's this term used around some of novelist Dave Eggers's writing – "a work of witness." Witnessing became such an aspect of our work together and then eventually with the public. You were inviting people to see you … and you them. In fact, I remember you saying when we did our first run in the theatre, "Can we turn on the house lights a little bit? Can we have at least a little bit of light so that I can see people's faces, their jaw lines, their cheekbones, their, like – can I see a little bit of their eyes?!"

KWM: Right.

AK: I always sensed that you wanted to be in conversation with your audience, that you wanted them to be consequential. When, in performance, you invite audience members to throw a hand up in the air or give a "hell yeah," *you mean it*. And when it does happen, you see it and acknowledge it. It's not one of those things that's like decorative icing for you, it's part of the substance of the encounter. I think it would be good for the reader to imagine that as they're reading the script.

KWM: Yeah.

AK: You taught me a lot about forms of realness onstage. I've always thought verbatim theatre is ... it's not that it's more real, but it certainly trades in the real, it engages with the real in a way that has an effect on an audience.

KWM: How do you mean?

AK: Just that you're telling the audience that the material has come from primary sources that aren't you, and you're conveying what those sources said, word for word. Playwright David Edgar once said, "Verbatim theatre wears its source on its sleeve." * I often say, it activates the conscience alongside the imagination because it tethers to the world in very direct ways. And you brought another level to it. When you asked questions in the show, and there are many questions in *Freedom Singer*, I remember observing, "Wow, he's ... actually asking the question to the audience. And he hopes they'll answer. He is interviewing them." It was an added layer, I would say, of reality to the encounter, which was both exciting and scary for its uncertain outcomes. You weren't just sharing the findings of your journey, you were continuing the journey with the audience.

KWM: You're making me think of that moment on tour when I was, "Oh shit, I'm in Alberta. I'm in a theatre with a bunch of subscribers, mostly white folks who did not come here for big questions," and I

---

* David Edgar, "Doc and Dram," *Guardian*, September 27, 2008, www .theguardian.com/stage/2008/sep/27/theatre.davidedgar.

was just ... I remember somebody laughed the wrong way, and I was like – I felt so unsettled.

AK: I remember that night.

KWM: What we're talking about right now is this sense of dialogue and reciprocity and the dialectic as performance, but also that we're *in communication*. Even if you're just witnessing here, there's something about the witness that also has a reciprocity to it. The witness is also filling your cup, as much as the person who's on the stage and who's supposed to be "performing." You're filling their cup, but also they're filling your cup. And it wasn't there in those moments with that particular audience.

AK: But you've since been back to that part of the country and have had positive experiences.

KWM: I made adjustments. I talked a lot with the audience. And people change, too, over time. It's really challenging to incorporate new ideas, we all sort of have a sense of resistance when something new happens, even if it's right, it's not what we have been doing. And when we have to change what we've been doing, that can feel really hard. There it is again: working on your own shit.

AK: I think that connects to, again, your interest in metaphor. Metaphors are to be interpreted, it's about turning over possibilities – and I think metaphors can make a lot of space for people, because they're open to multiple perspectives. They're poems. They can be so powerful alongside the kind of harder reality of verbatim, word-for-word testimony. But I must say, there is the flipside to that one night in Alberta, when I've seen white people in the audience, hands in the air, really relishing what you're doing. And I remember feeling uncomfortable with that dynamic too.

KWM: Right.

AK: I don't know how much that's me just projecting my own anxieties about what it means to be a white person who is affected by your experiences as a Black person, but I'm thinking about what it means for you as a Black person to say, "I've been denied a kind of history or access to history and I'm going to do something about it. I'm going to use my own ingenuity here and beat the system," and for a white person to be in the space, sharing in that victory of yours. Maybe that's not how they see it or feel it. But I'm confronted with so many questions: Am I allowed to participate in a Black man's journey? Is that for me? Is this a ritual or gift that I can even understand? Can I possibly get its import? Or is this not intended for me in that way? And is that okay. You know what I mean?

KWM: I think, again, part of what we keep questioning is: Are people coming to consume entertainment or have they come in for ceremony? Are they coming for the possibility of reciprocity? Are they coming for the potential to witness in a deeper way and be together in a deeper way? And it's hard to say. I think some people will get there during the course of a performance, some people already come ready to do that. Some are already there before we even say anything. And then there are some people who just are never gonna get it, they don't want it, and it's too confronting ... they feel like it's too much to ask.

AK: They feel prosecuted. We had a few white patrons of *Small Axe* who articulated that after the show. That they felt targeted.

KWM: Yeah, sometimes people don't want to move from where they're at.

TO BE IN RIGHT RELATIONSHIP

AK: Are we talking too much about white people?

KWM: I think what we're doing here is calling it out, referencing the elephant in the room. It's what you get with a Black man touring Canada, performing in a theatre space that is often held by white folks. It's what happens when a play like *Small Axe* turns audiences towards both Black stories of oppression and the way that white people relate to those stories. What does it mean to tell Black stories in these spaces?

AK: And the white gaze. What does it mean to disrupt it, even if initially, it's just by making it visible to the room? Did you know there would be an activist element to the work you were doing?

KWM: It wasn't in the front of my consciousness. I was just in the act of creation. I was surrounded by the material remnants of Black people and I didn't think much about what it would mean to share them. And yes, sometimes it's shocking to find yourself in front of an audience of bodies after you've been with a body of work. We live in bubbles, right?

AK: As [one of Project: Humanity's founders] Antonio Cayonne puts it: people are at different points in the social-justice curriculum. If it's a hundred books long, some people are on book two, some people are on book thirteen, and then there are others that have really put in the work and are further along in their understanding of power structures, white supremacy, the systems that surround us, of which we are a part.

KWM: Interesting, though. What you're talking about, it's in terms of understanding structural shit, but also it's something else. It's really relational. It's not all about the right words. You know what I mean? I don't think necessarily that a person needs to read the books, they just need to know how to be in *right relationship*. And how do you learn to be in right relationship? Well, you practise the practice of relationship. You know what I mean? And what that looks like is being together in a way that isn't transactional. It's about seeing the interconnectedness of things – and when I say "things," that's the animate or inanimate world. It's about showing up with your emotional body. What does it mean for an audience member to be vulnerable, to actually allow themselves to be seen and to feel? In that, theatre has such potential for social healing.

AK: There's lots in your practice that's about people accessing their vulnerability, communally. For instance, when you have people sing with you in your concerts, in *Freedom Singer*, regardless of their background, regardless of where they come from or what they believe. You ask them, "Can you just vibrate with me? You don't even have to open your mouth, just hum with me. Is that a possibility for us?" Music is such a gateway. You make a very good point around language: the way language fails a lot of people, and how people fail at language. And so how – not unlike metaphors or parables – how can songs be a way of democratizing information and experience and knowledge? And coming together?

KWM: Well, you notice how a bunch of old people like to sit around certain things ... you know what I'm saying? (*laughing*) Like snapping peas, playing cards, this is like ... I feel like I've had an Elder at some point say to me: "You can't have conversation if people's hands aren't busy." That's when the conversation can actually happen.

AK: A triangle, right? You, me, and our activity. You, me, and the song. You, me, and the theatre between us. And I think that's what theatre can manage, and music too – they give the audience and the artists a shared goal. Whether the goal is the story, or the song – it allows us to connect through a shared experience.

KWM: I do trust people because I trust myself. I trust the way that life works on a human heart, and I don't think anybody is able to escape if they're honest with themselves. You can't escape the way life works on a human heart. You can't. You can't escape the hard lessons that life is going to bring you. And if you really are attentive and present to what that means, I think that you can see your humanity reflected in lots of different places. By that I mean: finding yourself in the subject position of another, and seeing the world through their eyes. I think a lot of white men are not asked to find themselves in the subject position of another. If they're not cast as the hero, it all falls apart for them.

AK: It makes me curious about when you were imagining an audience for *Freedom Singer*. Who were you imagining?

KWM: Yeah, I've thought about this. When I lived in America, I did live in a much more monocultural space. Almost all my friends and associates were Black people, and so in that way, back then, I would've been speaking to them – 'cause that's my community. But now my community is not just them. Now my community is my partner Katherine, and it's her mom and dad and my niece, who all live in Australia. It's also my friends from Detroit, it's also my mom. It's also all the youth that I've worked with over the years in Indigenous communities, that I've become friends with. It's Jamaica. It's Uganda, it's Egypt. It's Germany. It's Barcelona. It seems disassociative for me to be like, "I'm only speaking to Black people." It's not actually true to what my heart knows. I could try to do that, but it would be fake. It strikes me as fake and it sounds like a cool thing to say, but in reality, it's actually about who you love and who loves you.

AK: Your audience is not a monolith.

KWM: No. And I'll say this – and this is also one of the things that I try to trouble as an artist, which is: *that's what racism is.* Racism is a flattening. It's a desire to make everybody who looks a particular way be the same way. And my understanding is rather, "Oh actually, no, we're very different, and that's awesome, and there are ways that we're similar, and that's also awesome." But if I go to Jamaica, if I go to Uganda, Senegal, Ethiopia, Somalia, Kenya, South Africa, Nigeria, Ghana, just alone in those individual countries, there are so many different languages, so many different cultures, so many different foods, so many different dances. So many different songs. And I start to feel weird when we start talking about the entire diaspora as one entity.

AK: We have to be specific, right?

KWM: *Freedom Singer* was my personal reflection in relationship to a body of music and my given experiences. I'm from Detroit. That's my contribution to the diaspora. It's not an attempt to be the diaspora.

THE WAYS THAT SHE MIGHT HAVE FELT

AK: Now, as a kind of closing to this midsection of the book, this *centre*, I wanna just ask about this *Freedom Singer* becoming part of a book. This whole creative journey started with a book. The author Karolyn Smardz Frost approaches you at a concert, hands you a book, and sets you off on a journey. And now *Freedom Singer* will be iterated as a book. What do you make of that?

KWM: The written word is really powerful and it's different than the spoken. I think with the written word, there's something longer about it. Longer in the sense that it's the same over time, and you visit it. Your interpretation of it can change, but the actual words of it ... they're always the same. With a book, I can return to it for meaning. With a book, I can find my own self in it, my different self, depending on when I pick it up. I love books, I love books, I love reading, I love, like, *stacks of them.*

AK: I mentioned earlier that pieces of art have lifespans with the public. A book shifts that lifespan and its potential. I want to remind you of something because I haven't looked at this in years, but I wanted to revisit our program notes for the premiere run of the show. Do you remember what your note was?

KWM: I don't.

AK: "Growing up, my mother used to assign me reading lists. In recent years, it's something I've started to do for myself. And I've been seeing more and more how the songs that I'm writing have been marked by the literary influences I've surrounded myself with. In some cases, these books and writers have been the very seed of inspiration." And then you list a bunch of books:

Citizen: An American Lyric by Claudia Rankine;

Between the World and Me by Ta-Nehisi Coates;

Stamped from the Beginning: The Definitive History of Racist Ideas in America by Ibram X. Kendi;

Strangers Drowning: Impossible Idealism, Drastic Choices, and the Urge to Help by Larissa MacFarquhar;

The Warmth of Other Suns: The Epic Story of America's Great Migration by Isabel Wilkerson;

Nobody: Casualties of America's War on the Vulnerable, from Ferguson to Flint and Beyond by Marc Lamont Hill;

Negroland: A Memoir by Margo Jefferson;

The Underground Railroad by Colson Whitehead;

Bound for Canaan: The Epic Story of the Underground Railroad, America's First Civil Rights Movement by Fergus M. Bordewich;

The Sellout by Paul Beatty;

and of course Karolyn Smardz Frost's I've Got a Home in Gloryland: A Lost Tale of the Underground Railroad, the book that launched this entire undertaking.

Isn't that interesting ... that that was your offering before people experience the show. The role that books have had in your trajectory.

KWM: It's also funny for me for you to have you read that, 'cause I was like, "Oh well, I did a lot of reading back when I didn't have a baby." (*laughing*) I used to read!

AK: Your ancestral grandmother Kizzy never got into the official record because her humanity and dignity were never recognized in her day and age. Is there anything for you around her being invoked in a book and people holding that name, her name, and her story in their hands?

KWM: Yeah, it's – again this kind of ancestral veneration, a lifting up. And also, in some ways, I feel like it's a critical tabulation. We talk about Kizzy quite a bit, but we don't actually really know Kizzy. Do you know what I mean? There's this way in which we are endowing possible thoughts and ideas to her, the ways that she might have felt. And again, part of it is because there's no record, part of it is because of a denial of access to the written word. And so, yes, there is something that feels really powerful and redemptive about somebody who would have very likely been denied access to reading and writing to then be venerated in the written word. I think that there's something that's really powerful about that.

Freedom Singer

Production History

Freedom Singer was originally developed by Project: Humanity. It was co-created by Khari Wendell McClelland and Andrew Kushnir with support from journalist Jodie Martinson.

Project: Humanity's *Freedom Singer* premiered on February 3, 2017, in Toronto, Ontario, at the Guloien Theatre, Streetcar Crowsnest, in association with Crow's Theatre and Urban Ink Productions with the following cast and creative team:

Cast & Crew

KHARI	Khari Wendell McClelland
CHORUS	Tanika Charles
GUITARIST	Noah Walker

Playwrights	Khari Wendell McClelland and Andrew Kushnir
Song Composer	Khari Wendell McClelland
Director	Andrew Kushnir
Research Dramaturge	Jodie Martinson
Set and Costume Design	Joanna Yu
Lighting Design	Oz Weaver
Sound Design	Debashis Sinha
Stage Management	Emilie Aubin

Freedom Singer toured nationally between February 2017 and February 2018 to the following communities: Regina, Calgary, Winnipeg, Montréal, Halifax, Ottawa, Guelph, Windsor, Gananoque, Edmonton, Victoria, Dawson City, Whitehorse, and (in partnership with Urban Ink Productions) Vancouver.

Characters

KHARI   The singer, songwriter, searcher, storyholder, storyteller

CHORUS   Khari's musical companion, also playing many of the people Khari meets in his travels through space and time

GUITARIST   Khari's musical support with guitar, percussion, and the capacity to trigger interview recordings and the voices of ghosts

Creators' Notes

Freedom Singer hybridizes two forms: verbatim theatre and music concert. Nearly all text has been drawn verbatim from carefully rendered interview transcripts. Khari's lines addressed to the audience emerged from interviews conducted by Andrew Kushnir. The encounters depicted in the play occurred between 2016 and 2017.

The play was originally performed by Khari Wendell McClelland, with the company of an electric guitarist and a Black female performer acting as Chorus.

Links have been provided for most of the songs.

In terms of punctuation:

- A slash (/) is used to mark the start of the next speaker's line (most often appearing before the initial speaker is done speaking). It makes for overlapping speech.

- Bracketed numerals like (2) or (5) denote the number of silent seconds that transpire between spoken text.

- Other punctuation marks such as commas, dashes, and ellipses are at times used non-grammatically in order to best capture the rhythm of the original speaker.

- There are passages in the play where, through a radiophonic sound design (see note "On sound" below), Khari shares the actual recorded voices from his documented journey. In some cases, Khari interacts with these voices as if in real time. At other times, the Chorus speaks in tandem with the voices and, in a few notable cases, embodies them in full character. Stage directions note these different modes as they occur.

- Stage directions in the script come from the play's first production and were conceived by director Andrew Kushnir.

On director Andrew Kushnir's production of *Freedom Singer*:

- On design: The set design by Joanna Yu consisted of a denim patchwork floor cloth inspired by the quilts of Gee's Bend. The upstage "wall" of the set included a large, frosted-glass panel onto which Khari etched his ancestral grandmother's name.

- On sound: The original production of the show had a radiophonic design created by designer Debashis Sinha. This was a kind of sonic collage that included archival sound bites, original interview recordings, compositions by Debashis Sinha, improvisational elements from guitarist Noah Walker, Khari's original songs, and Khari's reinterpretations of his ancestral music, which includes folk songs, songs of protest, and spirituals.

Songs

The songs of *Freedom Singer* lean into the aesthetics and styles of gospel, rhythm and blues, hip hop, funk, and others. Some songs, as noted below, have original lyrics and music by Khari Wendell McClelland; others are Khari's compositions as inspired by lyric fragments found during his research. A smaller number of songs are traditional pieces for which Khari created, or co-created, original arrangements.

Fleeting Is the Time
Written and arranged by Khari Wendell McClelland and including a passage from the traditional African American spiritual "Sometimes I Feel like a Motherless Child." www.youtu.be/qSoDE7Aypoo

Liberty Songs
Lyrics in part from Alexander McArthur, "*Tune*, Miriam's Song," and Joseph Thurston, "The Fugitive Slave Bill," both appearing in "Liberty Songs No. 2," *Voice of the Fugitive* 2, no. 2 (January 29, 1852), 4; song written and arranged by Khari Wendell McClelland. *Voice of the Fugitive* was Canada's first Black newspaper. www.youtu.be/v_J3BWkeoCI

My Mother Is Gone
Lyrics from an unidentified "coded message" song found in the Nova Scotia Archives; song written and arranged by Khari Wendell McClelland.

No More Auction Block for Me
Lyrics and melody received through a recording of William Riley in Helen Creighton Folklore Society's 2019 audio collection *Sankofa Songs, a Legacy of Roots and Rhythm: African Nova Scotian Songs from the Collection of Dr. Helen Creighton*; arranged by Khari Wendell McClelland and Ross Burns.

Never the Child Be Sold
Lyrics and melody received through a recording of William Riley in Helen Creighton Folklore Society's *Sankofa Songs, a Legacy of Roots and Rhythm*; rewritten and arranged by Khari Wendell McClelland and Juhli Conlinn. Originally titled "We'll Sell the Pig and We'll Sell the Cow, But Never the Child Be Sold."

Follow the Drinkin' Gourd
African American folk song, first published in 1928; arranged by Khari Wendell McClelland.

My Time Ain't Long
Written and arranged by Khari Wendell McClelland.
www.youtu.be/FhF7BdWcyfo

Oh, Dearest Mary
Lyrics and melody received through a recording of William Riley in Helen Creighton Folklore Society's *Sankofa Songs, a Legacy of Roots and Rhythm*; written and arranged by Khari Wendell McClelland.

Song of the Agitators
Lyrics in part from "Song of the Agitators," *Voice of the Fugitive* 2, no. 26 (December 16, 1852), 1, originally published earlier in 1852 in the *Ohio Star* (author unknown); written and arranged by Khari Wendell McClelland.
www.youtu.be/B36DJl12Kgo

Song of the Fugitive
Lyrics adapted from the 1852 poem "I'm on My Way to Canada" by Joshua McCarter Simpson, first published in Simpson's privately published collection *Original Anti-Slavery Songs*, from the same year; written and arranged by Khari Wendell McClelland. www.youtu.be/oEwB-6DZTOo

Roll On
Written and arranged by Khari Wendell McClelland.
www.youtu.be/6yCmgkVaKXw

Am I Not a Man and Brother?
Lyrics found in *The Anti-Slavery Harp: A Collection of Songs for Anti-Slavery Meetings*, compiled by William W. Brown (Boston: Bela Marsh, 1848), 5; written and arranged by Khari Wendell McClelland. www.youtu.be/WeTpHvfpAzA

1: Khari Wendell McClelland: "Sound the trumpet for me, so we can all be free."

2: Tanika Charles: "Leave the land of slavery and come across the line."

3: Noah Walker, Khari Wendell McClelland, and Tanika Charles: "Never the child be sold."

All photos by Dahlia Katz

Fleeting Is the Time

The **GUITARIST** *starts to play the opening lines of "Fleeting Is the Time" – a wet and electric sound. It has the quality of an invocation.*

The **CHORUS** *and* **GUITARIST** *sing from the stage.*

CHORUS and GUITARIST
Ooh, Ooh, Oo-oo-oo-ooh
Ooh, Ooh, Oo-oo-oo-ooh
Ooh, Ooh, Oo-oo-oo-ooh
Ooh, Ooh, Ooh.

Ooh, Ooh, Oo-oo-oo-ooh
Ooh, Ooh, Oo-oo-oo-ooh
Ooh, Ooh, Oo-oo-oo-ooh
Ooh, Ooh, Ooh.

KHARI makes his way through the audience and lands onstage. He addresses the room.

KHARI
I want to take a moment to thank you all for being here today. And for your witness. I want you to know that if you feel in a moment like you want to exclaim, say "Yes!" or "Amen!" or clap, that all your offerings are welcome. And if you understand me, say "Mmm-hm." One, two, three: "Mmm-hm!"

KHARI	CHORUS & GUITARIST
(*singing*)	(*singing*)
Sometimes I feel like a motherless child	Mmm, Mmm, Mm-mm-mm-mmm
You know, sometimes I feel	Mmm, Mmm
Like a motherless child	Mm-mm-mm-mmm
Sometimes I feel so all alone	Mmm, Mmm, Mm-mm-mm-mmm
And I'm a long way from home	Long way from home
Precarious set-ups made for mishaps	Mmm, Mmm
I ride the wagon bound for relapse	Mm-mm-mm-mmm
Lord, can I get an amen	Mmm, Mmm
And some handclaps	
For testimony, true story, ancient fabled allegory	Mm-mm-mm-mmm
The ones I've loved	Mmm, Mmm
The ones I've left behind	
They sometimes leave me crying and I don't mind dying, cuz	Mm-mm-mm-mmm
Fleeting is the time	Mmm, Mmm, Mmm
And I move across this land	Mmm, Mmm
Bumping into things that can't be held with hands	Mm-mm-mm-mmm
Only felt like parting words and final goodbyes	Mmm, Mmm
Cuz fleeting is the time	Mm-mm-mm-mmm
	Mmm, Mmm, Mm-mm-mm-mmm
Fleeting is the time	Mm-mm-mmm

KHARI	CHORUS & GUITARIST
No reasons why	Mmm, Mmm
No reasons why	
Who knows these things	Mm-mm-mm-mmm
Not me, not you, no king of kings, it seems	
Fools are we, sages, psychos	Mmm, Mmm
Jesters, pirates, and mystic winos,	Mm-mm-mm-mmm
Baby dolls and rusty nails, wind-blown trees and half-blown sails	Mmm, Mmm, Mm-mm-mm-mmm
Praying to the lord when all else fails	Mm-mm-mmm
Cuz fleeting is the time	Ooh, Ooh
We swing low like busted canopies	Ooh-oo-oo-ooh
Everything is wet and you are far out to sea	Ooh, Ooh
Yet I still heard you scream, "Somebody hold me"	Ooh-oo-oo-ooh
Cuz fleeting is the time	
Sometimes I feel like a motherless child	Ooh, Ooh Ooh-oo-oo-ooh
You know, sometimes I feel	Ooh, Ooh
Like a motherless child	Ooh-oo-oo-ooh
Sometimes I feel so all alone	Ooh, Ooh, Ooh-oo-oo-ooh
And I'm a long way from home	Long way from home

When I First Did That
(Records)

KHARI

I have an Ancestor who walked a mighty long way, in her bare feet, so that I could be alive. And could live a freer existence. And her name is Kizzy. And I'm wondering if you would do me the honour of saying her name with me on the count of three.

One... two... three...

> **KHARI** *gets the live audience to say his Ancestor's name.*

Thank you.

I say that name because it reminds me of who I am, where I come from, and, in some ways, where I'm headed. What's possible for me.

The first time I did that, I was at a community forum, in Vancouver. They wanted me to speak about where I come from and my relationship to the Commercial Drive neighbourhood and how I'd come to be there. And it came to me in a flash that I should say, "One, two, three... Kizzy."

For my family, Kizzy is our mythological matriarch. She is a rock in a stormy sea. She is that point of reference, when I feel lost, when I feel despondent, when I don't know where to turn, I often turn to her. Seems to me that if we all look back far enough, each and every one of us in this room has an Ancestor that's walked a thousand miles in their bare feet so that we can all be here.

If that resonates with you, let me see a hand. (*beat*) Now look around you.

Kizzy reminds me of the distance I have travelled.

I come from Detroit, originally. I'm not sure if you know, but Detroit is a little bit different than Vancouver. (*laughing*) Little bit. I remember when I first moved to Vancouver, the sound of a garbage truck dropping one of those big dumpsters on the concrete – making that big bang, that, initially, that sounded like gunshots to me. (I don't hear it that way anymore.)

I remember how much of a thrill it was for me to ride my bike all over Vancouver. All times of day. All times of night. No hands. Like, so different from when I was a kid: I literally couldn't ride my bike more than two or three houses in either direction. Those were the limits, because my mother and my grandmother didn't feel it was safe for me.

In Vancouver, in my community of Commercial Drive, a lot of people recognize me as the guy doing this... (*producing his ukulele and strumming a breezy tune*) playing his ukulele like this, singing to myself, with his head in the clouds. Yeah, and I didn't really do that in Detroit. (*interrupting his playing*)

My first job in Vancouver, it was as a florist working in a flower shop. And one of my favourite things to do was to take the petals off the roses when they were going, and to go out into the street and throw them out onto the footpath and... draw the customers in.

My job just before then, I used to work in a factory, a car factory in Detroit. At American Axle & Manufacturing.

Looking out at you now, it reminds me, the distance I have travelled.

KHARI takes a long moment to look out into the room, in silence. Then he cues the GUITARIST.

I gotta get comfortable.
I want to tell you a story.
And it's gonna take a minute.

KHARI removes his jacket.

A few summers ago, I'm in Lunenberg, Nova Scotia...

Frost

*The **GUITARIST** continues playing the root note of
"Liberty Songs" beneath **KHARI**'s text.*

KHARI

A woman comes up to me after my show. I'd just come offstage
playing a folk festival. She's wearing a T-shirt, dyed red hair, in her
sixties, your average folkie, you know – and she heard me talking
onstage about how I had a grandmother who came up through the
Underground Railroad to Southern Ontario. And that I was raised
in Detroit. And she hands me a book and says, "I wrote this book.
I think this might have relevance for you."

> *The **CHORUS** suddenly takes up the role
> of **KAROLYN**.*

KAROLYN

I wrote this book. I think this might have relevance for you.

KHARI

(*to the audience*) Yeah. And at first, I'm slightly dismissive just
cuz I'm just coming offstage so I'm pretty amped, and she's pretty
sober. And as quickly as she came, she disappeared. So I throw the
book in my bag without even looking at it.

A few days later, I pull it out of my bag, and the cover says: *I've
Got a Home in Glory Land*, by Karolyn Smardz Frost. And there's a
sticker on the front and it reads:

BOTH

"Governor General's Literary Award Winner – Non-Fiction."

KHARI
And I'm like, daaammmmn. I'm impressed. This lady won some prizes.

KAROLYN
Yeah I did.

KHARI
So I crack it open, I start reading this book, and of course I can't put it down.

The GUITARIST shifts the music slightly; the CHORUS hums a new melody.

KHARI
It tells the story of the Blackburns. This couple, Thornton and Lucie Blackburn, who escaped from slavery in Louisville, Kentucky, make their way up through Ohio to Detroit – a riot breaks out there – they head to Amherstburg, in Southern Ontario, eventually to Toronto. They actually started the city's first taxi service company. (1) I like to think of them as the Black Uber of their time.

So I'm really into the book, and I'm thinking about the Blackburns, and I can't help but think about Kizzy. I mean, this is the same journey: escaping slavery in the South, making her way through Ohio, then Michigan and Detroit and then Amherstburg, Ontario. It was amazing how parallel these stories were, and I thought to myself: These characters that Karolyn is describing in this book are likely the exact same people that my great-great-great-grandmother would have spoken to, that would have helped her as she made her way into freedom.

And as I keep reading the book, I start to notice these quotations, these poems – I think they're called epigraphs – at the beginning of a chapter – and, for some reason, as I read them I started to make up these melodies. In my mind. And suddenly I thought: Wait! –

The music cuts out.

Are these songs?

Are these the songs that Kizzy was singing?

A moment of silence and suspension. Then, KHARI starts to stomp the beat that's been taking shape in his mind.

Liberty Songs

KHARI
    Sound the trumpet over
    mountain and sea
    Proclaim glad tidings cause *the*
    slave is free
    Sound the trumpet
    Sound the trumpet for me

CHORUS
    Aaah

    Aaah

    Aaah

KHARI & CHORUS
    It's time we stand up and tell the truth to all the hungry, downtrodden, and forgotten youth. We waited long enough, the cheat is up, it's heating up, our time ain't long, it's time to do more than just sing songs.

    I want love, sacrifice, dedication, and relief for refugees without a nation. It wasn't that long ago when my great-gran was choked by yokes and at a loss for hope. But with the help of the Underground she made it safe and sound, went from lost to found. Hear the sound:

KHARI
    Sound of the people like
    thunder, are speaking
    Freemen are coming at
    Liberty's call
    The pride and the power of the
    tyrant is breaking
    Millions are rising
    Millions are rising
    Millions are rising from
    slavery's thrall

CHORUS
    Oooh-aaah

    Freemen are coming at
    Liberty's call
    Oooh-aaah

    Millions are rising
    Millions are rising
    Millions are rising from
    slavery's thrall

KHARI

Unfurl the banner and swell the chorus, time to recognize all the
ones who opened doors for us.

KHARI & CHORUS

Like Martin and Harriet, waiting for that chariot to carry us
home, working for justice in war zones. We still got work to do,
reparations overdue for catching hell from the prosperous few.
Some people say we'll get ours in the afterlife, but I'm in love
with this life, willing to cut through the strife. Singing like my life
depends on it, not for salary, but to be free. If you believe in me
like I believe in you and for the whole, not the few,

KHARI	**CHORUS**
Sound the trumpet for me	
So we can all be free	So we can all be free
Sound the trumpet for me	
So we can all be free	So we can all be free
Sound the trumpet for me	
So we can all be free	So we can all be free
Yeah, yeah, yeah	Yeah, yeah, yeah

*A shift. With the last chord of the song, we hear the
sound of a forest and bare feet walking in the woods. The
buzzing of cicadas creeps in and intensifies:*

KHARI

Kizzy.
Kizzy.
Kizzy.
Kizzzzzzzzzzzzzzzzzzzz ...

*A buzzing sound takes over. Another shift. The
CHORUS begins to hum. It is evocative of a woman
singing to herself on a bright and hot summer's day.*

Coates

KHARI

In his book *Between the World and Me*, Ta-Nehisi Coates writes: "Slavery is not an indefinable mass of flesh."[*] He makes vivid the diminution of the individual lives of those who were enslaved. Their distinct being. Their unique and fully human depth of feeling, thinking, relationship, aspiration, and capacity. He reminds us how their personhood has no fewer contours and peculiarities than our own. What do you enjoy? Who do you love? What irks you? Who do you know yourself to be? It is no different for them. For her.

"Slavery is not an indefinable mass of flesh."

KHARI & CHORUS
"Slavery is not an indefinable mass of flesh."

KHARI
"Slavery is not an indefinable mass of flesh.

"It is a particular..."

*But **KHARI** is interrupted.*

---

[*] Ta-Nehisi Coates, *Between the World and Me* (New York: Random House, 2015), 69.

Cathy on the Line

We hear a recording of **KHARI** *speaking with his mother,* **CATHY.**

KHARI

I got a question for you, Ma.

CATHY

Yeah.

KHARI

Do you know where she's buried?

CATHY

Who, Kizzy?

KHARI

Yeah.

CATHY

I don't know where Kizzy is buried, um... Cynthia is buried in Mount Clements.

KHARI begins to overlap with the recording, speaking to the audience.

KHARI

That's my mom, Cathy. (I interviewed her for this project.) She had me when she was nineteen, in college. And her counsellors told her she should drop out, but she did not listen. She persisted. She was a radical young person, used to take over radio stations, making sure they played enough Black music. She was also the

Class Jammer of 1972... and while I don't know exactly what that means... I have some ideas (she likely brought "the hype," brought "the party"). She's a community activist. And her work got her invited to the White House under two different administrations. She is very, very into African history. When I was a kid, I remember she gave me summer-reading lists. And at the time I found it... not the thing I wanted to do with my summer. But I'm grateful for it now. She still lives in Michigan.

Ma. Tell me about Kizzy.

The CHORUS takes on the character of CATHY and speaks to KHARI.

CATHY
Okay. Umm... Leona Dorothy who was, eventually became Leona Gainer, my grandmother, which was one of Cynthia's daughters, ummm... she was born in 1911 – she was a little girl when... (1) When she was a little girl Kizzy was still alive. Because she used to, umm, fight! She would get out, the kids would make fun of Kizzy because Kizzy had no legs. Kizzy had no legs.

The GUITARIST introduces the chords from "Song of the Fugitive," a song to come, under the following text.

KHARI
Yeah. Kizzy had no legs. She lost them in Canada. Froze them off living in some poorly heated barn in the dead of winter. At least that's what we know from our family stories.

So we don't have many facts about Kizzy. We don't have any records. What we know:
She escaped from slavery. Probably late 1850s.
She went to Southern Ontario.
She had two children with an Englishman. White guy.

She lived in a barn while he had a family in a house nearby.
Her eldest son, when he became old enough, strong enough, rowed
his mother and sister across the Detroit River back to the States.
Karolyn Smardz Frost was really intrigued by Kizzy's story.

The CHORUS has morphed into KAROLYN.

KAROLYN
Hm. That's interesting. She had no legs. This fact, this unusual fact
could be the very thing that helps you find Kizzy.

KHARI
That's what Karolyn says to me when I call her and tell her that I
got the grant to find Kizzy's music. Thank you, Canada Council.

KAROLYN
I know a couple of people with whom you may want to speak over
the next few months. You know, Khari, I think we met for a reason.
And we're being guided by something. A calling of some kind.
To turn ghosts into Ancestors. Right? All I'm saying is that I think
you might find more than music.

The CHORUS sings softly a reprise of "Liberty Songs."

CHORUS
Sound the trumpet
Sound the trumpet for me

*The sound of an airplane taking off. The sound of travel.
KHARI picks up his ukulele.*

Halifax / K'jipuktuk

KHARI

I have to say that, in my life... for reasons that I can't totally explain, it's been the women in my life that have been like a constellation above me, around me. Have been my guide. And I hold this awareness. That I don't have a lot of relationships where I feel a lot of safety and closeness with men. You know, where you're honoured and respected and seen. And so growing up, mostly it was my granny. My mom. And on this journey to find these songs, I was accompanied by a remarkable woman named Jodie Martinson.

> *KHARI plays "My Mother Is Gone" on his ukulele. The CHORUS has morphed into JODIE.*

JODIE

Khari, how are you going to know when you find a song that you want to pursue further?

> *The GUITARIST joins on guitar.*

KHARI

Jodie Martinson is a journalist. She's with the CBC and has asked to join me. She's going to document my journey, make a record of my search for this music. Jodie thinks she can help me find some record of Kizzy too, which would make a great story. We start in Halifax, K'jipuktuk in the Mi'kmaq language, at the Nova Scotia Archives. And I've got a good feeling about what we might find.

KHARI & CHORUS

My mother is gone
My mother is gone

My mother is gone
Into heaven my lord
And I can't wait behind

> *KHARI slings his ukulele on his back while the*
> *GUITARIST takes over the underscoring.*

KHARI
Jodie and I notice that a lot of the songs we're finding in the
Archives have the same sort of theme about "going up." Going to
heaven. Trying to find your family. Mother worship. And death.

There's always these multiple levels of metaphor in the songs.
Within the content, lyrically. It's hard to know exactly what people
were thinking... People are going to speak coded language about
the oppression they're facing and they will come up with creative
ways to thrive and survive and sometimes mock the oppressors,
mock the oppression they're facing, as well as deliver themselves
messages of hope. The songs are like maps.

KHARI & CHORUS
My mother is gone, my mother is gone, my mother is gone
Into heaven my lord
And I can't wait behind

> *The guitar swells and stops abruptly.*

> *We suddenly hear the sound of an archival recording:*
> *it is an excerpt from "Never the Child Be Sold,"*
> *featuring the voices of William RILEY and his daughter*
> *ROSE Mann, recorded on August 25, 1943, at Cherry*
> *Brook, Nova Scotia, by Canadian folklorist Helen*
> *CREIGHTON. It takes over the whole space.*

RILEY

Some said, years ago, that we were like cattle.

ROSE

Yes. (1) Will you sing that?

RILEY

Well I don't much care about singing my own, my own, mm-mm-mm, / way, it's too hard.

ROSE

But they're good, Papa! They're good, / Papa!

RILEY

I know, I know they're good, but do you / see, my folks had it so bad at one time...

> *KHARI speaks to the audience as the recording continues in the background.*

KHARI

His name was William Riley. From Cherry Brook, Nova Scotia. And Karolyn told me I'd find recordings of him here at the Nova Scotia Archives. He's just like... he's quite old and you can tell. In his nineties, I think. We find a recording of his from the 1940s in the archives of the Helen Creighton Collection.

And I just want you to take a moment, to think about the span of time. Is there anyone in this room born in the 1940s? All right. I want you to think that someone in 1940-something spoke with someone born before the abolition of slavery. Spoke with an enslaved person. It's in the living memory of people.

Now in the recording, his daughter Rose and Helen Creighton are trying to encourage him to sing these songs he knows. But he doesn't want to.

The recording takes the foreground again.

ROSE
But we, we have to take that and give it to the world, (*laughing*) yeah, yeah, in order to get the world up.

RILEY
Say what.

ROSE
They, they have to sing 'em so that we know 'em.

CREIGHTON
We remember them, the legacy.

ROSE
They remember how our foreparents was – that's right! They, they never stop singing in the States!

CREIGHTON
No.

ROSE
They *never* stop singing in the States. Them songs never die.

CREIGHTON
No, you're right.

KHARI

(*over the recording, to the audience*) Something very special is going to happen –

ROSE

And only the older generation can sing 'em.

CREIGHTON

Yes, that's / right.

RILEY

(*suddenly singing*)
No more auction block for me
No more, no more
No more auction block for me
Many a thousand gone
Jesus died on Calvary
Oh yes, oh yes
Jesus died to set me free
Thank him evermore...

Beat.

KHARI

This is a special recording to me. What a rare and powerful opportunity to hear someone from so long ago, someone who lived during American slavery. A lot of what I found out there were bits of lyrics in periodicals, suggested melodies. But here I found a full recording of this song.* And hearing Riley's voice... brought me to tears.

---

* Riley's recording can be found and purchased online on Bandcamp; look for "No More Auction Block for Me – William Riley," helencreightonfolk loresociety.bandcamp.com/track/no-more-auction-block-for-me-william -riley.

Constructing

*KHARI picks up his ukulele. Over the course of
this next sequence, we experience him working from
Riley's song fragment and progressively succeeding at
constructing his own iteration of the song.*

KHARI
No more auction block for me
No more, no more
No more auction block for me
Many a thousand gone

Jesus died on Calvary
Oh yes, oh yes
Jesus died to set me free
Thank him evermore

The GUITARIST joins.

No more auction block for me
No more, no more
No more auction block for me
Many a thousand gone

No more driver's lash for me
No more, no more
No more driver's lash for me
Many a thousand gone

The GUITARIST supports KHARI's riff on Riley's song.

KHARI	CHORUS
No no	Oooh
No no	Oooh
No no no no no	Oooh
No no no	Oooh
No more auction block for me	No more
No more, no more	No more
No more auction block for me	No more
Many a thousand gone	Many a thousand gone
No more crooked cops for me	No more
No more, no more	No more
No more penitentiary	No more
Many a thousand gone	Many a thousand gone
No more poisoned land and sea	No more
No more, no more	No more
No more early grave for we	No more
Many a thousand gone	Many a thousand gone

No more hypocrisy
No more, no more
No more child poverty
Many a thousand gone
Many a thousand gone
Many a thousand gone
Many a thousand – gone

No more
No more
No more
Many a thousand gone
Many a thousand gone

Many a thousand gone
Many a thousand ...
Gone

*We hear RILEY's voice again, a recorded encounter with
Helen CREIGHTON.*

RILEY
There, there, there was, there was this man, uh, and he was
in slavery. And he, he was a regular – he was a cotton picker.
A cotton, uh, makes – he used to pick cotton /

CREIGHTON
Yes /

RILEY
Of the slavery. And they would, um ... want the child. And there
would be, uh, all the slavers – holders – would roll along one night
to – to buy the child. To buy the child.

*This segues immediately into "Never the Child Be Sold."
RILEY's voice from the archival recording weaves
through it.*

Never the Child Be Sold

KHARI, CHORUS & GUITARIST
Oooh
Oooh
Oooh-Oooh
Oooh
Oooh
Oooh-Oooh-Oooh

KHARI
You can sell the pig
You can sell the cow
Never the child be sold
You can sell the pig
You can sell the cow
Never the child be sold

CHORUS
Oooh
Oooh
Oooh-Oooh
Oooh
Oooh
Oooh-Oooh-Oooh

ALL
Oooh
Oooh
Oooh-Oooh
Oooh
Oooh
Oooh-Oooh-Oooh

KHARI
You can sell the pig
You can sell the cow
Never the child be sold
You can sell the pig
You can sell the cow
Never the child be sold

CHORUS
Oooh
Oooh
Oooh-Oooh
Oooh
Oooh
Never the child be sold

KHARI
Horn will blow
Cotton does grow
Driver blow his horn
Horn will blow
Cotton does grow
Driver blow his horn

You can sell the pig
You can sell the cow
Never the child be sold
You can sell the pig
You can sell the cow
Never the child be sold

When you hear
The church bells ring
Dream in a dream

ALL
Oooh
Oooh
Oooh-Oooh
Oooh
Oooh
Oooh-Oooh-Oooh

CHORUS
Oooh
Oooh
Driver blow his horn
Oooh
Oooh
Driver blow his horn

Oooh
Oooh
Never the child be sold
Oooh
Oooh
Never the child be sold

When you hear
The church bells ring

Dream ...

KHARI	CHORUS
You can sell the pig	Oooh
You can sell the cow	Oooh
Never the child be sold	Never the child be sold
You can sell the pig	Oooh
You can sell the cow	Oooh
Never the child be sold	Never the child be sold
Never the child be sold	Never the child be sold
Never the child be sold	Never –
	Sold

Randy

We hear the sound of a phone number being completed, then a few rings. RANDY is a recorded voice that KHARI has a "live" interaction with. The effect of this exchange is that KHARI is on speakerphone with this elderly folklorist and historian.

KHARI

Hi Randy. I've put you on speakerphone because I'm sitting here with my friend and collaborator who is from the CBC, her name is Jodie Martinson.

RANDY

Hello there.

KHARI

And yeah, I was just curious to know, given your expertise in folk music, what kind of information or songs, or if you had any places to point me in reference to finding out about early Black Canadian music.

RANDY

Yes, indeed. Uh, you will want to...

KHARI

(*to the audience*) This is Randy – that's a pseudonym. He's a historian in Nova Scotia. Older guy. He recommends some collections I should look into, ones I was already acquainted with. He gave me a lot of sources. He seems to have an intense sense of ownership over the material.

RANDY
What specifically are you looking for?

Beat.

KHARI
Well, I'm looking for the songs my great-great-great-grandmother would have sung. We're on this search, this search for Kizzy, her story. And we're not making tons of headway, in the conventional sense, but as we're doing it, I'm trying to collect music, the songs that may have surrounded her. You know, maybe the songs are a different way of understanding her humanity.

Beat. Tension.

RANDY
Right.

KHARI
So I'm looking for songs that would have been sung by early Black Canadians in relationship to escaping the tyranny of slavery in the United States. And / I know that in –

RANDY
There's of course the vast majority of African Nova Scotians who were already here / before the advent of the Underground Railroad.

KHARI
Totally. (2)

Yeah, I'm hoping that in collecting these songs myself from people from Nova Scotia and Southern Ontario that I can provide something to Canadians Present and Future, you know, that Canadians provided space for people who were attempting to flee from tyranny.

RANDY

That's true but in quite a few cases, it wasn't a matter of – I mean, it's Great Britain first of all – because all this happened before there was a Canada itself. And a lot of times, helping runaway slaves, well, it was less than altruistic.

KHARI

Okay. (1)

Yeah, I'm aware of that, but the way it exists in the consciousness, in the mythology of Canadian people today. They don't really see that, they see –

RANDY

Well, I think the vast majority of Afri– the vast majority of Nova Scotians don't know the history of their own people.

KHARI

Yeah, but I guess what I'm thinking, the mythology that's around it is that Canada was good. That we did the right thing. Do you know what I mean? And there's maybe / value in that mythology?

RANDY

Yeah, I don't necessarily agree with you on that. But I see where you're coming from with that thought.

KHARI

Yeah, I don't know.

 Beat.

RANDY

You're saying you're compiling it. But what are you going to do with it afterwards?

KHARI

Well, CBC's documenting what's happening and they're going to
highlight, you know, the journey to find Kizzy and the collection of
the material, but I'm actually hoping to compile fresh recordings of
these old songs.

RANDY

Oh. I see. Yeah. Yeah. (3) Well. Good luck with the project.

A slight shift.

Suspended

*The **GUITARIST** gently underscores with the chord progression of "Follow the Drinkin' Gourd."*

KHARI

This guy I talked to, Roy – Roy is prof at the University of Detroit Mercy. White guy. Probably in his sixties. He's part of a network of nerds that study this stuff. He knows Karolyn Smardz Frost and he was very generous with his time and insight. He plays me a song:

CHORUS & GUITARIST

Follow the drinkin' gourd
Follow the drinkin' gourd
For the old man is a-waitin'
For to carry you to freedom
Follow the drinkin' gourd

KHARI

Roy says to me:

> *As before, **KHARI** interacts with the original recording of his interview.*

ROY

Yeah it is probably the most famous Underground Railroad song, but it's a fake. It's a twentieth-century invention.

KHARI

(*to the audience*) He's heard it sung as fact or talked about as fact in elementary school music classes, he's heard it played in the background of Underground Railroad exhibits in museums, he's heard it played or talked about in the background in documentary films on the Underground Railroad.

ROY

Never good. Because it is what Richard Dorsin the folklorist calls "fakelore." And what he means by that is there's no evidence that song existed before the twentieth century. The first record we have of this is in 1912.

KHARI

Hm. That's almost fifty years after the end of the Underground Railroad. So how is that a slavery-era song? Roy says to me, "People get so swept up in the feeling, the mythology of the Underground Railroad, and that's great, the Underground Railroad is something that suggests some possible models of cooperation, it says some positive thing about who we were. But we have to be careful, because the myth is powerful. It makes us feel things. And we sometimes forget about the facts, the reality of what's going on."

Remember this *Heritage Minute*?

> *KHARI* and the *CHORUS* jump into a heightened re-enactment of the 1991 Heritage Minute commercial "Underground Railroad." The *CHORUS* gives voice to *ELIZA* and the *YOUNG WOMAN. KHARI* plays Eliza's brother, *JOSH*, and eventually the *FATHER (Pa)*.

ELIZA

Pa should have been here by now. He's three hours late already. Pa ain't going to make it! One of them slave catchers got him! Something must've happened! I just know it!

KHARI
(*to the audience*) Do you remember this commercial? There's a
Black woman looking out the window. She yells at the white lady
who rushes over and starts holding her, trying to console her.

YOUNG WOMAN
Liza, you both made it past the border yesterday. We've all done
this before.

JOSH
He's our pa! He'll be here!

YOUNG WOMAN
He'll come. Let's pray.

ELIZA
No more praying!

KHARI
(*to the audience*) She runs out of the house.

YOUNG WOMAN
Liza!

ELIZA
No more praying!

YOUNG WOMAN
Liza!

KHARI
She's running through the town. White woman gives chase. They
see a carriage in the distance. Back in the church, a church pew is
being carried in. The white woman closes the big doors. Smile on
her face, like she's just completed a huge spy mission.

*The **GUITARIST** recites the following.*

NARRATOR
Between 1840 and 1860, more than thirty thousand American
slaves came secretly to Canada and freedom. They called it the
Underground Railroad.

KHARI
They crack open the church pew. And Pa spills out. The family is
reunited!

FATHER
Liza!

ELIZA
Pa!

JOSH
Pa!

FATHER
We're free!

ELIZA
Yes, Pa, we's in Canada!

> **KHARI** *and the* **CHORUS** *sit in that for a*
> *moment. A shift.*

KHARI
Yeah. We can get swept up in the feeling. The mythology of the
Underground Railroad. But we have to be careful.

Who was the hero in that commercial? Who was the helpless
victim? Who was weak? Who was strong and capable?

You know, I am aware of the facts.

When you read about the Blackburns in Karolyn's book... there
was this riot to break Lucie and Thornton Blackburn out of prison.
It was a plan that Black people put together and executed.
They're the ones that help get Thornton and Lucie out of prison.
Eight Black men help Thornton get across the Detroit River.
One of them gets shot.
The brown bodies took on all the personal risk.
Not the white people in that story.

A more rhythmic tone has set into KHARI's storytelling.

I am aware of the facts.
That the Underground Railroad wasn't this elaborate network of
superspies and church pews with secret compartments.
The Underground Railroad was actually, most often Black people
running for their lives.
And hoping for the best.

I am aware of the facts.
That Great Britain, British North America, Canada wasn't acting
out of altruism. They were nervous about their neighbours to
the south.
And wanted more bodies on that border, to defend them.

I am aware of the facts.
That those white Canadians were not waiting with open arms.
Most white Canadians at that time saw themselves as above
Black people.
In body.
Mind.
And moral capacity.
And this from people who were enslaving Black people just thirty
years before.

I'm aware that,
When Kizzy got to Canada,
She had two kids by a white man. A British man.
She didn't live in his house.
She lived in a sod hut on his property.
And she froze her legs off 'cause there was no heat.
And she went back to the States after Abolition. She didn't stay. For
whatever reason, she didn't stay.

I'm aware that the same Black people who were given passage to
Nova Scotia were later forced out of Africville.
I'm aware of the disproportionate incarceration of Black and
brown bodies in this country.
I'm aware of internment camps.
I'm aware of the fact that we're on stolen land.
That we're oppressing nature and animals and life.
I'm aware of the *Komagata Maru*.

It wasn't too long ago, I was making my way through Vancouver
and a police officer asked if I could come over for a moment.
He said:
"We just got radio that we've got a violent Black offender in the
neighbourhood; would you mind if we frisked you?"
And I complied because I'm aware of the facts. As he frisked me,
I overheard on the radio that the suspect they were looking for was
wearing a tracksuit.
I was wearing a suit and tie.
And so I asked the officer:
"If it was a violent white offender, would you stop every white man
that walked by?"
Would you stop every single white man who walked by?
He said:
"We'd do our best."

I am aware of the facts.

But what's the best way for maintaining my sanity and health and well-being so that I can be useful to myself and the people that I love.

Sometimes you need to improvise.
Sometimes you need to mythologize? No?
You know, people are always saying, "Take what you have and make something beautiful."
But sometimes what you have is nothing.

KHARI returns upstage to Kizzy's name and retraces it. He has yet to turn back to the audience before he starts speaking.

Where was she born?
What was she like as a girl?
How was she treated?
Who put into her head the possibility of running away?
How did she escape?
Who did she escape with?
What happened when she got to the Detroit River?
Was she scared?
Was there a ferry for her?
Did she have to swim?
Who took care of her once she got to the shore?
How did she connect with this British man?
Who was he?
What was their relationship?
How is it that she had two children by this man but didn't live in the same house as him?
Did he have a wife?
Why did she freeze her legs off?

A shift. A concerted move away from suffering. By this point, KHARI speaks directly to the audience.

What did she like to do with her time?
What were the things that put a smile on her face?
What was her favourite song? Her favourite flower?
What song did she sing to herself when she needed to find strength?
Were her hands like mine?
Did she find Ontario beautiful?
The Detroit River, was it beautiful to her?
How did it feel to be surrounded by her children and eventually her grandchildren?
Did she ever fall in love?
What were her dreams for her children and grandchildren and those that would follow?
Was I in her dreams?

Beat.

My Time Ain't Long

KHARI
My time is not long here
I gotta lay this body down
I got the hounds on my trail
It's the cross before the crown

We're gonna die anyway
Let's make a difference

ALL
Mm-hmm

KHARI
It's hard to tell what's real
It gets harder everyday
The direction is so clear
But obstacles are in the way

CHORUS
Mm-hmm
Mm-hmm
Mm-hmm

We're gonna die anyway
Let's make a difference

ALL
Mm-hmm

KHARI	CHORUS
I know that	
We in our silence	We in our silence
We been asking	We been asking
Mm-hmm	Mm-hmm
I know that	
We in our silence	We in our silence
We been praying	We been praying
Mm-hmm	Mm-hmm
I know that	
We, we been asking and praying	We, we been asking and praying

Time draws near
Form circle, draw plans
Choose love over fear
Sing our songs and join hands

We're gonna die anyway
Let's make a difference

ALL
Mm-hmm

KHARI	CHORUS
I know that	
We in our silence	We in our silence
We been asking	We been asking
Mm-hmm	Mm-hmm
I know that	
We in our silence	We in our silence
We been praying	We been praying
Mm-hmm	Mm-hmm

KHARI, GUITARIST & CHORUS
　　Spirits below and above
　　Show us some guidance and love
　　Cuz we're the lost generation
　　And we have lost all our patience
　　For your deception and lies
　　No more alibis

　　Spirits below and above
　　Show us some guidance and love
　　Cuz we're the lost generation
　　And we have lost all our patience
　　For your deception and lies
　　No more alibis

ALL
　　(*a capella and in unison*)
　　Spirits below and above
　　Show us some guidance and love
　　Cuz we're the lost generation
　　And we have lost all our patience

Ancestors

KHARI

I'm going to ask you again, on the count of three, to say Kizzy's name. One ... two ... three:

The audience says his Ancestor's name.

KHARI

Thank you.

> *In a very conversational way,* **KHARI** *then asks the audience to think of an Ancestor: a blood relative, a mentor, a positive influence on one's life ... And on the count of three, he has the whole audience utter the name of their person aloud.*

> *The room vibrates with voices and names and memories.*

> *He then, at random, invites two audience members to share the name of their respective person and why and/ or how they were meaningful to them.*

> **KHARI** *thanks everyone.*

Oh, Dearest Mary

KHARI retraces Kizzy's name with his hand. The
CHORUS takes the form of Kizzy's spirit, and sings
"Oh, Dearest Mary."

CHORUS
The hounds that beat upon my track
The master just behind them
I fear he will bring me back
Before I cross the line

Oh, dearest Mary, carry on for me
I'm doing all that I can do
To gain my liberty

Gently, she's standing on the shore
With her arms extended wide
Singing, "Leave the land of slavery and
Come across the line"

Singing, "Leave the land of slavery and
Come across the line"

Buxton – Cleata

KHARI
After Halifax / K'jipuktuk.

We head to Ontario. Would have been called Upper Canada when Kizzy was there.

We stop in Buxton, Southern Ontario. I'd read about Buxton in Karolyn Smardz Frost's book. She talked about how Buxton was like, you know, one of the best, like, most well-maintained Black settlements. And I heard the schooling was really good there. So good that the white parents used to send their kids to the Black school until finally the white school closed.

Had Kizzy stayed in Canada, she may have called Buxton home.

KHARI listens back to his original interview recording with Buxton choirmaster CLEATA Morris.

CLEATA
Do you sing "By and By"?

KHARI
Yeah.

CLEATA
What part do you sing?

KHARI
Tenor.

CLEATA

Boy could we use you!

*KHARI sings one line or two from Charles Albert
Tindley's early-twentieth-century hymn "By and
By." CLEATA hums with KHARI. The CHORUS
(embodying CLEATA) and KHARI take over live.*

KHARI

Cleata is ninety-one. She's been the choirmaster in Buxton for over
fifty years. We're both the descendants of those who escaped US
slavery. She's ninety-one. And I have to say... she's lookin' good.
She reminds me of my grandmother that passed. I miss her.

CLEATA

"Life can be beautiful if you live it right today." * You know
that one?

KHARI

No.

CLEATA

That's – (*singing a line or two from Dorsey's "Life Can Be
Beautiful"*). That's what the old choir used to sing with my mother
and uncle Charlie and all of them. Um.

KHARI

Life can be beautiful if you live it right today.
I notice a picture of you in the other room, recently taken. Looks
like you're doing something right. You play baseball at ninety-one!

---

*   From "Life Can Be Beautiful," a 1940 song by Thomas A. Dorsey.

CLEATA

Oh gosh! (*laughing*) Well it was, I never had so much fun in my life. And the referees and the announcers – I didn't get a hit the way you should, I struck out, the umpire said: "You want to hit the ball?" So he tossed a ball up and I hit it, I didn't even attempt to get on the cart, they had golf carts to take us to first base, but my great-niece, she took off, she ran first base and somebody else was running for somebody else and the young kids, she was eight and it was the eight-year-old kids, they were our runners. This little eight-year-old runnin' for me.

We gotta run for each other. Ain't that what you doing?

KHARI

Collecting songs. Trying to understand where my family comes from.

CLEATA

That what you're doing.

KHARI

Well I want to carry on the music.

CLEATA

Good for you. And that's what's needed.

KHARI

It's funny because I think about how important music was to our people and how we probably wouldn't survive without it.

CLEATA

We couldn't. And they didn't.

Listen.

You're a young man and I sincerely wish you the best and that you're going to continue this line of music. We can't let it die.

KHARI
No I don't want it to.

CLEATA
Would you sing something for me? Something you wrote?

KHARI
I would love to.

KHARI breaks from CLEATA and looks out.

KHARI
But it'll involve the participation of my audience.

Song of the Agitators

KHARI

(*to the audience*) Will you sing it with me? Just sing: "Mm-hm."
One more time: "Mm-hm."

KHARI	ALL
"Cease to agitate," we will	
When the slave whip's sound	
is still,	
Mm-hm	Mm-hm
When no more on guiltless limb	
Fetters cut the circlet grim	
Mm-hm	Mm-hm
When no more hounds a thirst	
for blood	
Scouring the thorny	
Georgian wood	
Mm-hm	Mm-hm
When no more a mother's	
pleading prayer	
Quiver on the southern air	
On that day we shall be	Oooh, Oooh
Family, equal-born, and free	Oooh
Dawn will come, night shall cease	Oooh, Oooh
We'll rejoice, mind at ease	Oooh
Day for which we work and wake	Oooh, Oooh
That's when we'll cease to agitate	

KHARI	ALL
That's when we	That's when we …
That's when we will cease to agitate	That's when we …
That's when we	That's when we …
That's when we will cease to agitate	That's when we …
That's when we	That's when we …
That's when we will cease to agitate	That's when we …

Here we are today	
Still pushing for equal pay	
Mm-hm	Mm-hm
And these Treaty Rights don't hold	
Shiny like Judas's gold	
Mm-hm	Mm-hm
The stain of blood remains	
A mother's only son slain	
Mm-hm	Mm-hm
Youth cryin' out for more	
Continually ignored.	

On that day we shall be	Oooh, Oooh
Family, equal born and free	Oooh
Dawn will come, night shall cease	Oooh, Oooh
We'll rejoice, mind at ease	Oooh
Day for which we work and wake	Oooh, Oooh
That's when we'll cease to agitate	
That's when we	That's when we …
That's when we will cease to agitate	That's when we …
That's when we	That's when we …
That's when we will cease to agitate	That's when we …
That's when we	That's when we …
That's when we will cease to agitate	That's when we …
That's when we	That's when we …
That's when we will cease to agitate	That's when we …

Amherstburg

KHARI listens to the original audio reflection he recorded upon his arrival in Amherstburg, Ontario, with Jodie Martinson.

KHARI

(*as recorded*) I am feeling like a really nostalgic feeling. Like, I don't know, I just feel all of the, I don't know, a lot of emotion and the power of, like, connecting with, um, where you come from. And yeah, I don't know, it kind of feels like a powerful recognition, reckoning.

(*to the audience*) That's what I say to Jodie as we pull up to the Freedom Museum in Amherstburg. Karolyn had told me about this place. They've got all kinds of archives there, collections, family binders, family trees, newspaper clippings. If there's any one place where I could find something out about Kizzy, this is it.

We meet Terran, who's one of the curators. She knew we'd be coming. Terran tells us that she's going to go into the archives, which are still in the process of being digitized, to find anything she can on Kizzy. She leaves us with DeShawn, our tour guide. In his twenties... there was something very cute about him. Just kinda like a, like his first summer job. That kind of vibe.

In a weird way he reminds me of my little brother Adam.

Freedom Museum

KHARI steps offstage and starts working
his way through the room, as if giving a tour.
He embodies DESHAWN.

DESHAWN

So I'm going to take you on a tour! We could do this a couple of ways. We could start in the main building now, or we could go back outside and start in the church, and then I'll take you back around to the main building.

A shift to the church. There is a marked change in light.
And a vibration in the air.

DESHAWN

This is Amherstburg's African Methodist Episcopal Church, or AME Church for short, built here in 1848 by fugitive slaves from the US.* So this was the ending point to the Underground Railroad. And maybe a place where your great-great-great-grandmother Kizzy might have actually come.

Now, the original features of the church are these church pews and, uh, the central beam in the ceiling.

Music starts for "Song of the Fugitive."

---

*   Full name: the Nazrey African Methodist Episcopal Church National Historic Site of Canada, part of the Amherstburg Freedom Museum.

KHARI

(*as himself, to the audience*) Yeah, Deshawn. I walk around and Deshawn tells me about his lineage, about both sides of his family. He knew so much about his family. He even had a photo of a freedom seeker from his family named Harris. And I gotta say, I was a bit jealous. I wish I knew that much about my family. I said to him, "I wonder if Kizzy and Harris ever kicked it, you know, went to church, or shared a meal or something." He was like: "I dunno. Maybe." I walk. I walk around the church.

Song of the Fugitive

KHARI

    I am on my way to Canada
    That cold and dreary land
    The burdens of slavery
    I can no longer stand

    I said
    No no no no
    No

        A shift. **DESHAWN** *is indicating to various objects in*
        case displays.

DESHAWN
In the museum, you've got African instruments.

African shoes, masks.

Here we have shackles, leg shackles.

If you're a small child growing up in slavery and you're given a leg
shackle – if they didn't take it off over a certain amount of time –
your skin would actually begin to grow over top of these. There's
actually stories of people from slavery having to get these removed
and usually having to lose the leg.

KHARI
    I now embark for yonder shore
    Sweet land of liberty
    The vessel will bear me over
    And I shall then be free

No more to dread the auctioneer
Nor fear of master's frowns
No more to tremble from the baying of the hounds

No no no no

Oh, oh Father won't you help me
Oh, oh Father won't you set me free
Oh, oh Father won't you... help me

> *A shift.*

DESHAWN
So this here, this piece is actually probably their most prized piece
in the museum. This is called the lashing ring, which was taken off
a property nearby and the tree that this was actually lodged into,
what was called the Bloody Whipping Tree. A slave owner from
near here, on the Canadian side...

So this stake would actually stick into the tree and the ring would
be out and you'd tie slaves there. This, this was taken off his
property.

Would you like to hold it?

> *KHARI, reluctantly, holds it. The accompaniment of
> "Song of the Fugitive" courses under this moment.*

KHARI	CHORUS
Yes! I am safe in Canada	Yes!
My soul and body free	
My blood and tears no more	
Shall drench the soil of	
Tennessee	

KHARI
Yet how can I suppress the tear
That steals from my eye
To think of my friends and kindred
As slaves to live and die

KHARI	**CHORUS**
No no no no	No no no no
No no no no no	No no no no no
No no no no	No no no no
No	

Oh, oh Father	Ooooo
Thank you for setting me free	
Oh, oh Father, thank you for	
helping me	Ooooo
Oh, oh Father, thank you	

> *The music stops.* **TERRAN***, as played by the* **CHORUS***,
> steps onto* **KHARI***'s platform, folder in hand.*

KHARI
Hi Terran.

TERRAN
Hi.

KHARI
(*referring to the lashing ring*) You don't mind if we take a look
at this?

TERRAN
No I really don't.

KHARI
It's a powerful piece.

TERRAN
It really is, I think it's one of the most powerful in the museum.

KHARI
Yeah, I mean just talk about the layers of history. So this was on the Canadian side?

TERRAN
I think unfortunately Canada has a habit of excluding some of the darker parts of our history and this is just one of the examples. Yeah. And I mean the freedom story's so great, so of course we want to share that, but unfortunately this also gets lost.

KHARI
Yeah. Did you find something about Kizzy?

Beat.

TERRAN
Okay, so we looked through the Smith family binders to see if there was anything there. As you suggested we looked up last names Bloodsoe, Cobb as well. Looked at some family trees and did some work looking into the census, and again, unfortunately, we couldn't quite place anyone.

So, you know, we're still looking. We love doing this sort of thing and we're hoping, if you guys maybe find the next step, we'll be able to help you again.

But Khari, I did dig up some music stuff for you. Yeah, these are lyrics from songs. "Follow the Drinkin' Gourd" is probably one of the most well known so that's in there, but there are a few others as well. I'll be happy to copy those for you.

KHARI
Thank you. That's great.

Beat. Silence. (3)

KHARI
Um. I'd like to see the church again, if that's okay, before we go.

TERRAN
Of course.

The Church – Roll On

KHARI re-enters the church. That buzzing, cicadas in hot summer, creeps in along with the sound of his shoes as he walks on the church's hardwood floors.

KHARI
Kizzy.

After a moment, he starts addressing his Ancestor. What starts as a quietly sung prayer takes on epic proportions.

KHARI
I sang my song to the river in the valley below
In the hopes it might wash away my sorrow
And as I walked away I heard the river clearly say
"Roll on, my son, roll on"

KHARI	CHORUS & GUITARIST
Roll on	
Roll on!	Roll on!
Roll on	
Roll on!	Roll on!
You could sigh	Sigh
You could cry	Cry
You could almost die	Almost die
Roll on	
Roll on	Roll on

ALL
Even though it's hard to know
Roll on, hold on, roll
Even though it's hard to know
Roll on, hold on, roll on

KHARI
I sang my song to the river in the valley below
In the hopes it might wash away my sorrow
I did as I was told
By the people of old
Roll on, my son, roll on

ALL
Even though it's hard to know
Roll on, hold on, roll
Even though it's hard to know
Roll on, hold on, roll on
Even though it's hard to know
Roll on, hold on, roll
Even though it's hard to know
Roll on, hold on, roll on

We hear those crunching footsteps in the forest again.
KHARI listens to the footfalls.

A shift.

Detroit

*A city soundscape. A recording of **KHARI** singing to a song on a car radio, as captured during his research trip. **KHARI**, onstage, has a rose in his hand.*

KHARI
I think it's important for me to paint the picture round.
Detroit is not one thing.
Detroit is a place where I get a certain part of my dignity from.
It's Black men in suits and Black women in pastel dresses with heads held high on their way to Easter service.
Where I first learned about music.
Marcus Belgrave who played trumpet for Ray Charles.
Detroit is where I was first loved into existence.
My mom and grandma,
Jonathan and Kenny in elementary,
Kyle, Reggie, Ronnell in middle school and high school.
It's also where I get my flavour from.
The rakish angle on my hat. My undone laces.
Some of the most joyous moments of my life are contained there.

But Detroit is also this:

It's my grandmother pulling me into a closet or under the bed when there's gunshots.

When I was a kid, I couldn't ride my bike off of my block. Actually, I couldn't ride past two houses in either direction. So it pushed me to kick it with my granny's friends. I remember Eda and Slim. I hung out with Mississippi and Georgia, the Great Migration from the South. Listened to their stories. And those stories live inside of me.

All those Elders are gone. And the neighbourhood isn't the same.

Jodie Martinson, she wanted some video footage of where I grew up. I didn't think it through. Me in this car with two white people, one has a huge camera. And we're rolling through, and on the corner, there was a drug dealer and he started mean-mugging me, started giving me the screwface. And I got it. I was disrupting his business.

So we got out of there.

Detroit is a hard place. And I think I've always been softer.

I think some part of me was always yearning for that place that would let me be more freely myself.

Cathy

We hear **CATHY**, *Khari's mother, in their original interview recording.*

CATHY

There was never a time that I can recall, I don't recall a time when I didn't have music in the house. There was just like always music and uh, my mom loved to do two things. Sing. And dance.

KHARI

Hey Ma, I remember sitting together, me and Granny would have a little jam session. I remember she would put on a fancy hat. And I would put on a polyester suit. She'd put some Howlin' Wolf on the record player. And she'd put two glasses on the table and she would fill my cup with apple juice and hers with whisky.

The **CHORUS** *overlaps with* **CATHY***'s audio and then takes over, live.* **KHARI** *hands* **CATHY** *the rose he's been holding.*

CATHY

Yeah.

Beat. After some time:

KHARI

You remember when I called you at work, when I was seven in Lancing?

CATHY

Yeah, I was at work and a group of grown people in a car were calling you the N-word. Oh I remember that. Very well.

KHARI

And um. What was it like for you to hear me call you when I was seven and to hear me say these adults have, like, you know, basically verbally assaulted me.

CATHY

I felt outraged. Absolutely outraged.

KHARI

I just remember I called you, you were consoling me, and then at a certain point you said, you said, "Stop crying," and I was like, "Whoa," and you were like, "Stop crying," you said something like, "This is part of the way that life is," you said that sometimes people aren't nice, sometimes they're mean.

I remember when we first moved to Detroit and I remember going over, you know, me being really soft and not hardened to what life would be like in Detroit and I remember you telling me that you used to, like, put, have me in a mental bubble, you used to, like, put me in a bubble –

CATHY

Because you had to go to school, so what I would do, the only way I could protect you was to mentally, like, put a shield around you and a bubble.

So if you can imagine, um, if you think of it in current terms, like, if you had a dome, if it was the military or a war, and you have a shield or a dome that helps to protect you from rockets or whatever being sent... to blow you up. It was my mental dome, a shield, a prayer, I guess, in a sense, but using visualization. So I would see you in my mind wrapped in a bubble that protects you.

I'm your mom, you'll always be in that bubble.

*KHARI takes a breath before venturing into his
confession.*

KHARI

It's what pains me about, about knowing that you are here.
Because I feel like my quality of life, my relative safety is pretty
guaranteed when I'm at home in Vancouver. And I don't feel like
that when I'm here. And I look at you and I look at Adam – and
it makes me wish Kizzy and her kids never would have went back
across the river, to be quite honest.

> *Beat.*

I went up to Buxton and I'm hanging out with Aunt Cleata and
her friends and I'm thinking they're living until one hundred years
old almost all of them, living super old, they don't – they're not
walking around with all this anxiety of violence, all this fear, all
of the real lived consequence of having to deal with violence on a
regular basis, and so I really can't help thinking to myself I wish
Kizzy would have never left.

I know that I ran. I know I ran.
I ran off to Vancouver eleven years ago.
And I feel like I was ghosting on you and Adam.
But there's something about...

When you're far from home
You can reinvent yourself
Try on new things
Maybe get closer to yourself.

And the world feels big for me right now.
I feel like I'm riding my bike with no hands
And I'm throwing petals at the world... and drawing people in.
The distance I have travelled.

But sometimes, I'm out there, and I wish you could see it the way I do.

Sometimes, I wish Adam could see what I see.

Who I've surrounded myself with.

I sometimes wish you could feel the things that I'm feeling.

I wish you didn't have so much worry.

So much anxiety.

Wish you could feel more happiness.

And more joy.

But

More than anything

I

I just wish there was a place where we can all be together.

> *Silence.* (4)

CATHY
Well. Yeah. I understand.

> *Another silence.* (3) *A shift.*

> *We start hearing the recordings, the layers of voices ...*
> *people and spirits that* KHARI *has met: Cleata,*
> *Randy, Terran, Rose, Riley, and others. It culminates*
> *in* CATHY's *recorded voice.* KHARI *picks up*
> *on his mother's recording, and starts echoing her,*
> *word for word:*

KHARI
So if you can imagine, um, if you think of it in current terms, like, if you had a dome, if it was the military or a war, and you have a shield or a dome that helps to protect you from rockets or whatever being sent ... to blow you up. It was my mental dome, a shield, a prayer, I guess, in a sense, but using visualization. So I

would see you... and I see you... and I see you... in my mind
wrapped in a bubble... in a bubble that protects you.

Beat.

(*to the audience*) There's always these multiple levels of metaphor
in the songs. Within the content lyrically... it's hard to often know
exactly what people are thinking... People are going to speak
coded language about the oppression they're facing and they will
come up with creative ways to thrive and survive and sometimes
mock the oppressors, mock the oppression they're facing, as well
as deliver themselves messages of hope.

The songs are like maps. Right?

Am I Not a Man and Brother?

KHARI

Am I not a man and a brother?
Ought I not, then, to be free?
Sell me not to one another
Take not thus my liberty

KHARI	**CHORUS & GUITARIST**
And oh	Oh
Saviour	
Oh	Oh
Saviour	
She died for me	Oooh
As well as thee	Oooh
Oh she died	
Oh she died for me	

Am I not a man and a brother?
Have I not a soul to save?
Oh, do not my spirit smother
Making me a wretched slave

And oh
Have mercy
Oh
Have mercy
Don't let me die a slave
Don't let me die a slave
Let me feel
Let me feel a freeman's grave!

CHORUS
Yes, thou art a man and a brother
Though we long have told thee nay
And are bound to aid each other
All along our pilgrim's way!

KHARI	**CHORUS**
Oh	Oh
Be welcome	
Oh	Oh
Be welcome	
Join with us	Ooo-oooh
Join with us to pray!	Ooo-oooh

ALL

Join us
Join us
To pray

Join us
Join us
To pray

Join us
Join us

KHARI
To pray

THE END

How Do We Get from Here to There?

AN ESSAY BY **KHARI WENDELL McCLELLAND**

> may the tide
> that is entering even now
> the lip of our understanding
> carry you out
> beyond the face of fear
> may you kiss
> the wind then turn from it
> certain that it will
> love your back   may you
> open your eyes to water
> water waving forever
> and may you in your innocence
> sail through this to that

> —LUCILLE CLIFTON, from "blessing the
> boats," *Blessing the Boats: New and Selected
> Poems, 1988–2000* (2000)

How do we get from here to there? And by that I mean: How do we become what we are longing to be? How can we become wiser, more generous, kinder, more thoughtful, stronger, more flexible? I think the path is iteration. Trying over and over again, making mistakes, revising, regularly adjusting our tack and trajectory. A metaphor I like to use to describe this existential journey is that of walking. As infants, many of us learned to walk driven by the will to explore ourselves and our relationship to the world around us. It is often a clumsy and hazardous effort. What is remarkable is that those who witness these events are often drawn to cheer for the one who tries with great effort as they fail, falling victim to gravity, over and over again. One way of understanding what is happening is failure. Another way to understand what is happening is iteration. What is walking after all? Isn't it the graceful act of catching yourself over and over again as you fall? Shouldn't this be the way we understand the practice of art making? Shouldn't we have permission to try, to find grace as we stumble forwards, compelled by curiosity and the desire to understand ourselves and our relationship to the world around us? That is what art is for me when I allow it to be. That is what *Freedom Singer* was and is for me.

it·er·a·tion /ˌidəˈrāSH(ə)n/

noun

1. The repetition of a process or utterance.

   1.1 Repetition of a mathematical or computational procedure applied to the result of a previous application, typically as a means of obtaining successively closer approximations to the solution of a problem. [...]

—*New Oxford American Dictionary*, s.v. "iteration" (2010, 2021)

I'd never embarked on a journey like *Freedom Singer* before. I'd never written a suite of songs, I'd never been a part of creating a documentary, I'd never helped create a documentary theatre piece, and yet I felt compelled to do so. *Freedom Singer* was not a testament to my will. I was guided and compelled by forces larger than myself – Karolyn

Smardz Frost's book, Jodie Martinson's support,[*] Ancestors, and myriad others who cheered me on. The journey wasn't without its challenges. Sometimes fear crept in. I had days when I questioned if white audiences deserved the authenticity of my heart. I wondered if my mom would see my work as an honour for our family. I questioned if my story was important enough to share. In the end, none of my doubts were equal to my enthusiasm for the learning journey. My enthusiasm was a kind of grace that was gifted to me. I know what it is like to have to struggle through a project without the buoy of enthusiasm or grace. I was blessed with the opposite and for that I am grateful.

In some ways, it's easier for me to speak to the impact of *Freedom Singer* by giving thought to the work I created right after it. My subsequent theatre project, *We Now Recognize*, which premiered in February 2019, was born of my curiosity concerning the nature of apology – What is owed to the aggrieved? – and how that related to the nation-state and my patrilineal family relationships. *We Now Recognize* was the next step on my iterative journey, a way to deepen my exploration of self, my family, and the nation. *Freedom Singer* had a deep focus on the women in my life, whereas *We Now Recognize* was an opportunity to explore the dearth of male connection and love in my life. Much like *Freedom Singer*, I wanted to confront the unspoken and underlying truths that undergird my experience and the national context surrounding it. When I think about reckoning with histories national and personal, I think of writer Kiese Laymon. He encourages us to be honest about where we have been in order to get to where we long to be. "The most abusive parts of our nation obsessively neglect yesterday while peddling possibility. I remember that we got here by refusing to

---

[*]   Jodie Martinson's 2016 documentary, also titled *Freedom Singer*, was part of the CBC documentary series Absolutely Canadian. Interested readers may wish to consult "Searching for the Soundtrack of the Underground Railroad," CBC Radio, February 19, 2016, last updated November 18, 2016, www.cbc.ca/radio/tapestry/journeys-to-a-new-life-1.3453607/searching -for-the-soundtrack-of-the-underground-railroad-1.3453636.

honestly remember together." * *We Now Recognize* was my attempt at honestly remembering together. I set out again doing things I had not done before, using new methods of inquiry and communication that were illuminating in ways I could not have imagined. I used Gullah quilting, hip hop, and the artist Arthur Jafa as aesthetic inspiration. A centrepiece of *We Now Recognize* was four letters I wrote as a way to communicate longings that had never been uttered. I wrote a single letter to each of the following: my grandfather, father, younger brother, and an unrealized child. I went across the country, retracing a path I previously tread with *Freedom Singer*, reading these letters, singing songs, quoting literature and national apologies. I was practising courageously the revelation of my heart's longing. I was acknowledging and saying out loud what I longed for but had been too afraid to utter for fear that it would not be realized. This is in line with *Freedom Singer*'s underlying desire for deeper connection with family and place – "I just wish there was a place where we can all be together." So much of my life's work is iterative of generational, familial, and national reckoning. I find that juxtaposition of the familial and the political undeniably captivating, and as a consequence I iterate it through arts practices in order to understand it. Trying again and again to get closer to truth, revelation, and grace. A way of walking that might be helpful to me and "all my relations."

With both *Freedom Singer* and *We Now Recognize*, at times it felt awkward and I questioned my willingness to air the laundry of my family. Part of me wanted to yield to my family's dynamic of secrecy. I look back now and think perhaps I should have done some things differently. What I wouldn't change is the attempt at getting closer to my heart's yearnings. *Freedom Singer* enabled me to find new ways to work through challenges and share ideas. Ways that are unique to the medium of theatre. As a songwriter, I could capture a great deal, but theatre allowed me the capacity to go deeper. It gave me a wider palette to paint with. *We Now Recognize* allowed me to further explore metaphor and

---

*   Kiese Laymon, *Heavy: An American Memoir* (New York: Simon and Schuster, 2018), 231.

aesthetic possibilities. The two plays were gateways on my artistic and iterative path. They enabled me to iterate and reap meaningful rewards. It is safe to say many people are reaping the rewards.

Sharing this work, over and over, before hundreds of audience members, was like a prayer or incantation, and many opportunities flowed out of this. Within a year of sharing *We Now Recognize*, I ended up receiving something I had longed for my whole life: discovering and meeting my biological father and two siblings. I also ended up becoming a father. I've since become closer to my brother and grandfather. All of this is almost too much to believe. Is it possible that by sharing the truth of my heart with supportive witnesses I was able to receive what I was longing for? Part of what I revealed in those letters was all of the disappointment and loss associated with those relationships –

> It is okay for me to share my disappointment. It is okay that I still want a healthy blended family and a loving father. I want to know my siblings. I want to know your wife. It has taken a long time to be okay; to be okay with wanting what I might never get and finding a way to be okay with that. It feels better than lying to myself or pretending that my desires don't exist. The desire to love and be loved by you. I'm imagining there are some things that you haven't allowed yourself to feel and imagine.
>
> Your son, Khari

– and part of what I revealed was a longing for iteration, reunion, and the possibility for my family to love in a new way (as articulated in the letter to an imagined child of my own) –

> ... love is worth it. It makes us vulnerable, but it also makes us strong. I will keep on loving you in spite of my doubts and fears. I will do it for us and for the generations of men who have been kept away from love.
>
> Your Father.

Freedom Singer and *We Now Recognize* are works that attempt to "honestly remember together" in order to iterate towards more loving and liberatory ways of being in the world.

I'm writing these words with the hope that it might encourage us to be more audacious in iterating, trying, failing, succeeding, and revising over and over. This is especially important in a society that often seeks to keep things in a status quo. *Freedom Singer* was an attempt at revising history, mine and a national narrative. How can we find the courage to be more honest with ourselves about where we have been and what our grieving hearts are yearning for? I think that through this iterative process there is healing on the other side. Healing that could help tend to old wounds and our current afflictions. This is the generational work of the community – relational work. I am nudging us to follow what our deepest humanity is begging of us, for a world stuck in a holding pattern that could really use some revision, some iteration. It is less about the perfection of the single offering and more about how it might lead you to your next iteration as an artist and human being, and what that might mean for our world. *Freedom Singer* and *We Now Recognize* were steps on my life's journey. My next theatre work is a play, entitled *Confluence*, that focuses on the intersections and shared histories of African-descended people and Indigenous Peoples on Turtle Island. Work that deserves my courage and willingness to keep falling forwards, finding grace through my efforts, the efforts of the Ancestors and all those who've walked alongside me, cheering and lovingly guiding me along the way. Can you hear that? The ruckus excitement of the world awaiting your next steps, waiting to cheer for you in order to see the world born anew, again and again.

Lucille Clifton's "blessing the boats" is from *How to Carry Water: Selected Poems of Lucille Clifton*. Copyright © 1991 by Lucille Clifton. Reprinted with the permission of The Permissions Company, LLC on behalf of BOA Editions Ltd., www.boaeditions.org.